DEPARTMENT OF HEALTH

The Children Act 1989 and Family Support:

PRINCIPLES INTO PRACTICE

Edited by
JANE GIBBONS

London : HMSO

ISBN 0 11 321549 5

Contents

List of Contributors

Professor Antony Cox, Department of Child and Adolescent Psychiatry, Guy's Hospital, London

Ruth Gardner, formerly Senior Development Officer, National Children's Bureau; now Divisional Manager, The Children's Society

Jane Gibbons, Senior Research Fellow, Social Work Development Unit, University of East Anglia

Dr Pauline Hardiker, Senior Lecturer, School of Social Work, University of Leicester

Ann Lewis, Senior Research Associate, Social Work Development Unit, University of East Anglia

Professor Roy Parker, Department of Social Policy and Social Work, University of Bristol

Dr Andrea Pound, District Clinical Psychologist, The Royal London Hospital

Dr Christine Puckering, Lecturer in Clinical Psychology, Department of Psychological Medicine, University of Glasgow

Dr Lyn Quine, Senior Research Fellow, Centre for Research in Health Behaviour, Institute of Social and Applied Psychology, University of Kent

Wendy Rose, Assistant Chief Inspector, Social Services Inspectorate, Department of Health

Teresa Smith, Lecturer in Applied Social Studies, Barnett House, University of Oxford

Dr June Thoburn, Senior Lecturer, School of Social Work, University of East Anglia

Jane Tunstill, Adviser, National Council for Voluntary Child Care Organisations

Helen Westcott, Research Officer, Public Policy Department, NSPCC

Ian White, Director of Social Services, Oxfordshire

Acknowledgments

Acknowledgments are due in particular to Carolyn Davies and Wendy Rose from the Department of Health; Jan Pahl and Daphne Statham from the National Institute for Social Work; Professor Spencer Milham from the Dartington Social Research Unit, who chaired the original Seminar; and Connetta Smith who played a vital role in the organisation of the whole project. The Rowntree Foundation commissioned the work reported in chapter 7; and The National Society for the Prevention of Cruelty to Children that in chapter 6.

Foreword

Wendy Rose

Genesis of the Book

Like so much of the Children Act itself, this book, and the original seminar from which it sprang, began as a small idea which gained currency and support the more that the views of others were sought, was amended and developed in the process and finally arrived in a larger and more comprehensive form. Over a year ago Jane Gibbons, Jan Pahl and Carolyn Davies began to discuss how the findings of complementary, recently completed Department of Health research studies might be disseminated. A small seminar was suggested. It became evident, however, that with the implementation of the Children Act and the significance of family support services, it would be valuable to reflect on how the messages from the studies might be used both to promote service development and to indicate areas for further research. This is not a well researched area and it was hoped that some valuable insights might be shared.

The Department previously held a seminar on research findings on under-fives services which led to a publication, distributed to all social services departments. It was decided to follow a similar model and to focus this time on studies of family support services, other than day care, and to seek to stimulate debate and interest.

The Children Act 1989

The Children Act places a general duty on local authorities to safeguard and promote the welfare of children in their area who are in need and, subject to that duty, to promote the upbringing of such children by their families. The new emphasis in Section 17 is for local authorities to work with the family and child in the family home and for local authorities to work with or facilitate the work of others.

This is reinforced in Section 27, with the new duty on other agencies to assist social services in the performance of their duties. This is a vital opportunity for local authorities to influence others in the way they work with families (partnership in all aspects) and to encourage multi-disciplinary working and mutual understanding between all agencies.

The new provisions of the Children Act enable a range of services such as accommodation not to be seen as a breakdown in preventive services but as a positive measure of family support. They allow for the development of imaginative and flexible services in partnership and in support of families, with the users' views fully taken into account and services assessed against the welfare check list of Section 1. Such developments have a relatively recent history.

Putting Family Support into a Longer Time Perspective

We have been reminded on a number of occasions recently by Roy Parker, Jane Gibbons and Bob Holman amongst others that "the idea that the state had some responsibility to assist children in their own homes—to prevent family breakup and consequent removal of children—is relatively recent". Rescue and removal were the focus of the Poor Law and of pioneering Victorian child care societies. It is helpful to place the current provisions of the Children Act in a longer time scale and to note that it was not until the Children and Young Persons Act of 1963 that children's departments were given statutory powers to engage in preventive casework and give material assistance under Section 1.

This provision, however, was found to have opened the floodgates to demand; referrals increased for work with children in their own homes and, as Jane Gibbons has written:

> 'Prevention' was to prove too narrow an objective to encompass the wider range of provision that began to develop in response to demand, especially after the introduction of unified social services departments in the early 1970s. The continuing use of the term, necessary to provide statutory justification for local authority activities, began to lead to confusion.

As Jean Packman has pointed out, the service was quickly forced on the defensive.

The Barclay Committee, in its report on community social work in 1982, appeared to suggest that social workers might withdraw from 'the rescue of casualties' in favour of identifying and strengthening natural sources of help in the community. But the evidence to support this was thin and social workers were reluctant. It is hardly surprising then that the Short Committee looking at social services in 1984 found that "there" is not really a clear understanding of where preventive effort should be concentrated or how... At the moment there is a certain miasma of vagueness".

During the preparation for the Children Bill, the term 'prevention' was recognised to be inadequate and the Review of Child Care Law identified two main aims for local authority provision for families with children: to provide 'family support' to help parents bring up their children; and to seek to prevent admission to care or court proceedings except where this is in the best interests of the child. Thus the Children Act with its provisions in Part III and in Schedule 2 aims to provide a clearer framework for local authorities to support families in need.

It is worth noting that this has been underpinned over a number of years by the Department of Health's policy to target its own grant-making capacity and its special initiatives to encourage the voluntary sector to offer family support services and to encourage a partnership approach to working with the voluntary sector. Grant aided organisations include Home Start, Newpin, The Family Centre Network, Playmatters and Family Service Units.

Policy in the Department of Health has been both to address child protection needs and at the same time to encourage the development of services to support families in need.

The Obstacles to the Development of Family Support Services

Putting resources into prevention, into family support services, has often required a supreme act of faith rather than rational explanation by Directors of Social Services in the last decade—and then such services have often been precarious and prey to budgetary cuts. While some social services managers have been prepared to set up family support services, I have heard a number of reasons for not doing so, which include some of the following:

- **The paramountcy of 'priority' work**, however priority is defined. This has meant responding to referrals of child abuse and to families at immediate risk. Not only has this unbalanced child care services but it has led in some cases to registration on the child protection register becoming the threshold for access to services.

- **Financial considerations** and the difficulties of demonstrating cost effectiveness. It is easier if projects do not need capital investment.

- **Political considerations** and the unacceptable overtones of community work which still exist in some authorities: suspicions that working with and empowering local people may eventually lead to local action and an increase in demands or an undermining of local democracy. For example: a social services department wanting to appoint a worker to work with the residents of a local housing estate, undergoing contortions of language to gain political agreement—not even 'outposted' could be used, and eventually the post was called 'social worker at large'.

- **Effectiveness** and the problems of evaluation, the difficulties of demonstrating success or effectiveness of projects or services, given the multiplicity of other factors which might have prevailed. For instance, was the drop in child care referrals to a social work team from a local housing estate due to a year's involvement on the estate of a community worker or were there other reasons?

- **Is it social work?** Should social services departments be providing the service? Family support or preventive services are often marginalised in terms of status and career progression in social services departments, and not integrated into mainstream services.

- **Developing coherent policies, strategies and services is difficult.** The diversity of potential services poses problems of how to target them and how to provide them. For example: home based support to families, day care, respite care, packages of services, community centres, drop-ins, community action or directing energy at changing the policies of other council departments or even central government—a manager's nightmare.

- **Tension between the need to be flexible** and responsive to individual needs and yet not to create services which become institutionalised and out-of-date. For example: one authority built a large all-purpose day centre for a local neighbourhood which rapidly became a white elephant and unused.

- **Short term perspectives of social services departments.** It is sometimes difficult to argue for services which will have a longer term pay-off but will not have an immediate effect on demand for acute services.

- **Voluntary organisations' grants,** which are vulnerable to short term financial considerations and which are exposed to all the difficulties of demonstrating effectiveness.

This is not an exhaustive list of the obstacles cited by social services departments and yet it demonstrates why some of them have been reluctant to apply managerial time and resources to developing family support services.

The Fears and Hopes for the Way Ahead

Inevitably, while the Children Act has been so widely welcomed, there have been fears that non-acute, family support services will not be developed. These fears have been clearly expressed by Jane Tunstill on behalf of the In Need Implementation Group, set up to promote Part III of the Act. The Group's Report (1991) argues:

> Family support services have to be provided at an early stage, and generously, in order to be effective. It is often not possible to tell in advance which families are at greatest risk. There is evidence that early support reduces risk although little research has been funded to consider the costs and benefits of such service. Such services need not be more expensive than intensive intervention at a later stage. However, where savings are the primary or only consideration, more universal, low-key provision is neglected for fear of encouraging demand. Eligibility and access to services should not be determined by narrow, administrative definitions of need.

Jean Packman and Bill Jordan have also warned that the problems which emerged from the 1963 Act have uncomfortably close parallels with today:

> 'Support' in the Act is not intended as a universal service for all but one selectively applied to 'children in need'... demand for services is certain to outstrip supply. The danger must be that the assessment of 'children in need' will, perforce, become another rationing device albeit of a more sophisticated kind than the ones used in the sixties.

Amidst these fears there is hope. As Packman herself says:

> Perhaps the best hope for progress lies in the many examples of good practice that already exist and which the Act simply reflects and builds on. Amongst these would be flexible respite care for disabled children that might be more widely applied; family centre models based on partnership and participation and high quality direct work with children.

Through this book we are seeking to present to you the findings from recent research of examples of good practice. We hope the book will encourage debate about how local authorities can provide and develop services, and how researchers can assist in evaluating such services. We intend to distribute the book to all social services departments and to voluntary child care organisations, to widen and stimulate the debate further.

Note: References are listed in Appendix B.

Introduction

Jane Gibbons

This book had its origins in a Seminar held at the National Institute for Social Work in November, 1991. The Seminar papers, together with others specially commissioned, have been collected in this volume because it is believed that they could be useful to a wider audience interested in family support services. The volume is particularly aimed at managers in local authority, health and voluntary services who are responsible for drawing up and implementing policies which will, over time, make a reality of the new provisions for family support in the Children Act 1989. The Guidance on the Act has stressed that,

> The local authority as a whole should have an agreed and approved policy on family support services for children and their families... Steps should be taken to ensure that such a policy is developed and agreed, involving all relevant departments and organisations in the process. It should include arrangements for monitoring and implementation (DH, 1991, para 1.8).

The book is not intended to be used as a practice primer or a training manual. It brings together in a convenient and more accessible form new findings from recently completed British research projects into the development, maintenance and effects of different kinds of family support. It provides examples of new ideas and new services which have been carefully evaluated. It aims to promote thought and debate about key issues in the development of family support provision.

Section 17 of Part III of the Children Act gives local authorities a general duty to safeguard and promote the welfare of children in need and to promote the upbringing of such children by their families (where this is in the child's interests). Section 17(10) states that a child is 'in need' if:

(a) he is unlikely to achieve or maintain, or to have the opportunity of achieving or maintaining, a reasonable standard of health or development without the provision for him of services by a local authority;

(b) his health or development is likely to be significantly impaired, or further impaired, without the provision for him of such services; or

(c) he is disabled.

The Guidance on the Act states that:

> The definition of need . . . is deliberately wide to reinforce the emphasis on *preventive* support and services to families. It has three categories: a reasonable standard of health or development; significant impairment of health or development; and disablement. It would not be acceptable for an authority to exclude any of these three—for example, by confining services to children at risk of significant harm which attracts the duty to investigate under section 47. (DH, 1991, para 2.4. My italics)

Thus local authorities must not have policies that restrict support services to families who are already in severe difficulties that pose a risk to the children, or to children on the verge of care, or returning home from care. They must identify the extent of 'need' (using the definitions in the Act) and then make decisions on the priorities for service provision. They will be open to challenge if those priorities exclude services for children who fit one of the statutory categories of 'need'.

Departmental guidance (Para 2.11) states that local authorities will have to ensure that a range of services is available to meet the extent and nature of need identified within their administrative areas, including day-care provision for pre-school and school age children, services to support and improve the strengths and skills of parents in their own homes, a vigorous foster care service and a range of placements. Part 1 of Schedule 2 to the Act lists other provision that should be available to families, such as advice, material help and family centres. Local authorities must work in partnership with other providers and they must publicise the availability of such services as well as monitoring and evaluating them.

This book does not attempt to deal with the full range of services that can be viewed as family support. It does not, for example, consider day-care, nor accommodation nor fostering. It focuses in particular on three types of provision: locally-based projects and family centres that are intended to increase supportive resources in areas with many social needs; services more specifically geared to parents who are identified by others or themselves as in some way falling below acceptable standards of care for their children; and services for families containing a child with a disability.

Key Issues

A number of key issues run through the different chapters. First, there is the theme of partnership between social workers and other professionals, parents and children.

Then, there is the view of family support as involving something more than material or practical benefit—important though that is in itself. 'Good parenting', which has been defined as predictable, available, sensitive and responsive caretaking within a structured and responsive home environment, is the key to promoting the welfare and optimal development of children. But parental functioning is influenced by a variety of forces, of which the most important, apart from the personality of the parent and the characteristics of the child, are stresses and supports in the surrounding environment (Belsky & Vondra, 1989). Maltreatment, in this perspective, is the outcome of accumulated risk factors accompanied by a deficiency in support or in compensatory factors. It is the total pattern of stresses and supports that enhances or undermines parenting capability, and there is considerable evidence of positive effects on aspects of parenting when sufficient social support is available, as well as negative effects when social support is lacking. Family support provisions under the Children Act, therefore, have an important part to play in 'buffering' the effects of stress on vulnerable families.

Third, there is the issue of who should receive provision, or, in current jargon, how provision should be targeted. The contributors to this volume show remarkable agreement that, while authorities have to decide on priorities for their service provision, this is not the same as restricting services to 'heavy-end' cases. For example, children in poor families, living in overcrowded, bad housing or in bed and breakfast accommodation, need services under the family support provisions of the Act to help them achieve "a reasonable standard" of development.

A fourth common issue concerns who should be involved in the actual provision of services. Several chapters show that residents in local communities, trained volunteers and parents themselves are extremely effective in a whole range of provision and that family support services should not be dominated by professionals from social services, health or education. Local residents can take on management responsibilities for local family projects (chapter two). After training, volunteers can provide high-quality advice and befriending services and they can provide direct services to children through creches and playgroups (chapters one, two and three). In general, lay workers may be as or more effective than highly qualified professionals in providing enriched social support to hard-pressed young families. Parents themselves may become highly effective therapists in a model of service developments where skilled specialists teach skills to front-line professionals (such as health visitors), who in turn train parents (chapter seven). However, there may be limits to what can be asked of lay workers and volunteers, and most would not want to carry the main responsibility where parenting problems are compounded by severe personality or mental health problems or where they involve the infraction of legal norms. The strength of innovative family projects is that they can reach families earlier, give more open-ended and sustaining support and reach out more effectively in a less stigmatising way than official services. They are not a cheap substitute for needed therapeutic services. (Halpern, 1990). Further, there is a need for a core of professional support to maintain the volunteer group (chapter three).

Another important issue (dealt with particularly in chapters eight and nine and in Workshop 1) concerns the need for co-ordination and co-operation between different parts of the local authority (social services, education and housing) and between local authority, health and social security services. At present not all these agencies appear to be moving in the same direction. Further difficulties are apparent in the relationships between the statutory and voluntary sectors (see, for example, the Summing Up) though this volume also contains many examples of successful partnership. Many of the problems are bound up with the issue of finance and the straitened circumstances of most local authorities and voluntary organisations alike. The underlying problems of lack of resources are recognised in the book but are outside its remit.

Important for all forms of family support provision is the need to ensure that due attention is paid to religious, racial, cultural and linguistic factors. This theme is recognised throughout the book and specifically treated in Workshop 2. However, higher priority needs to be given to these issues both in policy development and in future research.

Finally, a principal theme of the book is the contribution that empirical research can make to developing effective practice and policies in relation to family support. In a cycle of research and development, research skills are needed first, to document the extent of 'needs', how they are perceived by family members and the gaps in existing provision. Monitoring and evaluation then go hand-in-hand with service developments to assess how far goals are being met, in what aspects services are effective and where they are falling short. This information is fed back to the responsible service providers, who modify provision in the light of the new information. In this book, the evaluation of the Newpin project (chapter three) provides a good example of the cycle. Independent research found that while Newpin was highly effective in involving and helping parents with severe personal difficulties, the programme (as it was then running) had less effect on actual parenting skills. This information allowed Newpin to modify its programme so that, without losing the components which had been demonstrated to be extremely effective, new components could be added to address the problem of deficient parenting skills more specifically.

Structure of the Book

The book is divided into three parts, preceded and followed by the introduction and summing-up delivered at the original Seminar. Part 1 contains chapters by Teresa Smith and Jane Gibbons concerned with locally-based community projects—demonstrating an approach that is unselective and universal within particular neighbourhoods containing many young families under pressure. Part 2 is concerned with selective provision. Chapter three, by members of the Newpin research team, describes and evaluates an important voluntary project addressing the needs of families referred because of serious difficulties, including risk of significant harm to children. Thoburn and Lewis describe means of involving parents in child protection work and of making a reality of 'partnership' with family members in these testing circumstances. Part 2 ends with a section on provision for families containing a child with disabilities. Pauline Hardiker introduces the section and provides a framework for policy development: encouraging examples of progress in local authorities and the voluntary sector are cited in illustration. Helen Westcott shows the need to address the vulnerability of disabled children by increasing their range of choice and access to ordinary services as well as by providing special services. She describes a successful example of innovative family support provision strongly based on partnership with parents and on inter-agency cooperation. Lyn Quine describes and evaluates a new service for families containing children with serious disabilities who also had sleeping difficulties. The results showed the success of the service in training health professionals and parents (who acted as therapists), and in reducing stress on families.

Part 3 is concerned with policy development within agencies. Ruth Gardner draws out the lessons from a research and development project in two local authorities, and Jane Tunstill summarises the available information on how policies are being developed in local authorities, sounding some cautionary notes. The conclusions of the Workshops that formed part of the original Seminar are summarised in Appendix A. A short reading list is contained in Appendix B.

References

Belsky, J. & Vondra, J. (1989) Lessons from child abuse: the determinants of parenting. In Cicchetti, D. and Carlson, V. (eds.). *Child Maltreatment* Cambridge: Cambridge University Press

Department of Health (1991) *The Children Act 1989 Guidances and Regulations: Volume 2: Family Support, Day Care and Educational Provision for Young Children* London: HMSO

Halpern, R. (1990). Parent support and education programs. *Children and Youth Services Review*. 12, 285–308

PART 1

Studies of Open-Door Provision

CHAPTER 1

Family Centres, Children in Need and The Children Act 1989

Teresa Smith

Family centres are now 'official'. In the Children Act 1989 they appear for the first time in the list of services for children and families that local authorities are required to provide as 'appropriate to children within their area'. This paper presents a commentary on different types of family centre and on the term 'children in need', drawn from preliminary results of a study carried out in 1991/2 of 125 users with young children in six family projects established by the Children's Society in different parts of the country.

What are family centres and why are they worth study? Holman (1988) and De'Ath (1988) provide a useful working definition of three different types: the client-focussed centre which works with referred clients and has a strong 'professional/client' ethos; the neighbourhood type of centre typically located in areas of high social need, which offers a broad range of activities and encourages user participation; and the community development type characterised by collective action, local control, and workers offering indirect support to community groups rather than direct provision of services. The new legislation presents a broad view of family centre clientele and activities: according to the Children Act, centres may provide 'occupational, social, cultural or recreational activities ...advice, guidance or counselling; or ...accommodation' to children, parents, carers, and anyone with 'parental responsibility' (Schedule 2, part 1, para. 9). The Department of Health's guidelines (1991) make it clear that provision—whether local authority-run or voluntary—should be available to a 'wide range of families' and 'children of all ages', rather than restricted to children defined as 'in need', and includes services ranging from intensive casework, parenting skills, family functioning and packages for families with children in need, to day care, playgroup sessions, toy libraries, employment and skills training, marriage guidance, child health clinics, and 'out of school' clubs (paras. 3.18-3.24).

The aspect of family centres most worthy of study in policy terms is the potential they offer for flexible services of interventions for families, whether on the basis of individual definitions of need or on the basis of a geographical approach to what the Department of Health's guidelines term (para. 3.23) 'poor environment'. In this study we considered the consumer response to, or user view of, a range of services and approaches in the six centres. Recent studies have provided good descriptions of family centre organisation and activity (Ferri, 1991), use observational techniques to study adult-child interaction in 'client focussed' family centres (Calam and Franchi, 1987), explore preventive work with families in different contexts (Gibbons, 1990), report on consumer views in one centre (Cigno, 1988), and analyse the concept of partnership (Daines, 1990). This study, in the tradition of consumer research, treats users' views not just as symptoms but as valid descriptions in their own right. It is therefore proper to investigate users' definitions of need and to scrutinise whether professionals' and users' views match or not. This chapter explores two questions raised in the study:—

• Who used the six family centres?

• How did families define their own experience while bringing up young children in the often highly disadvantaged neighbourhoods served by these projects?

Who uses Family Centres?—A User Profile*

Who uses family centres? We start with a 'user profile', reporting briefly on ethnic identity, family structure, health, income, and geographical mobility.

Almost all of the 125 users interviewed were women. This reflects one of the dilemmas for such projects—the mismatch between the label 'family centre' or 'family project' and the fact that care of young children is seen to be women's responsibility. When we asked whether partners used the centres, replies like the following—'It's for me and the kids'; 'He doesn't like being with other women'; 'That's women's—I wouldn't even suggest it!'—reinforce the stereotype of family centres as women's work, places for women and children.

This study gives a largely white view of family centre work. We asked respondents their place of birth and ethnic identity. Five of the six centres catered for largely white neighbourhoods. 104 of the 125 users (83 per cent) had been born in Britain, and 78 per cent described themselves as 'white'. The one inner city project was the only centre with a significant black identity. With just nine of the 25 respondents born in Britain and three describing themselves as

---

* This paper is based on information from questionnaires carried out with 125 users in six projects. For the purposes of this chapter, users are treated as one group except where indicated otherwise. Percentages refer to the whole group.

'white', this project accounted for almost all the users in the total sample born outside Britain, as well as 'black British', and those describing themselves in terms of identity as 'black', 'Indian', 'Pakistani', 'Bangladeshi'. A quarter of the families using this project came from East Africa, being Indian or Pakistani by origin.

The 125 households in the sample contained 281 children between them—an average of 2.2 children per household, although many households contained only one child and some contained up to six. Lone parents headed thirty-five of the households (28 per cent). The proportion of lone parents in the sample ranged from one in twenty families in one project to almost half the families interviewed in two other projects. More than one child in four (29 per cent) was growing up in a lone parent household. Again this ranged from 5 per cent of the children in one project's households to 48 per cent in another. One way of considering levels of income and household circumstances is to ask whether households are 'waged' or not. 64 per cent of the households had a wage of some kind coming in; 36 per cent did not. But only one in five (20 per cent) lone parent households had a wage coming in, compared with almost eight out of ten (79 per cent) 'couple' households. Lone parent households were more likely to be unwaged than 'couple' households in all the projects.

Another way of considering income is to ask about the adequacy of material circumstances. Only 25 per cent of our families considered they had adequate levels of income, compared with 75 per cent who 'always' or 'sometimes' had financial difficulties. This ranged from 100 per cent of the households in one project to 60 per cent in another. It was no surprise to find unwaged households describing themselves in difficulties (62 per cent 'always' and 29 per cent 'sometimes'). However, two in three of the eighty households with a wage coming in also described themselves in difficulties. We would expect to find more lone parent households in financial difficulties, and this was indeed so in all six projects: 88 per cent of the lone parents said they were 'always' or 'sometimes' in difficulties. However, more than two in three of the 'couple' households also described themselves in difficulties. Although these figures are based on 'self-report', rather than derived from data on actual household income, they nevertheless indicate problems of low pay and part-time or insecure employment.

An example from one of the six areas studied illustrates the difficulties facing many families. Eight of the ten households interviewed were 'unwaged' (interestingly, in the two 'waged' households it was the women who were the wage earners); nine of the ten households (including lone parent households, and the two households with the women wage earners) were largely or entirely dependent on benefits, and were 'always' or 'sometimes' in

financial difficulties. This was an area of both high unemployment
and low wages—indicated again by the fact that three of the ten
women interviewed had partners on government training schemes
rather than in work.

Here are some examples from interviews in this area. 'It's a
struggle all the time.' 'We don't go out—we can't afford it.' A
woman with two children said the family project had arranged a trip
and a group holiday that year: 'we wouldn't have had a holiday
otherwise.' One lone mother with two children said she always had
difficulties with the bills. Both children had severe health difficulties,
as did the mother. The family centre had helped her with food
vouchers and had lent her household equipment, and one member
of staff had lent her money. 'They're very generous.' 'You can't
afford to buy the children's shoes... help with furnishings—I
haven't even got any curtain rails...'

In another project, where one quarter of the families was headed
by a lone parent, most found it very difficult to make ends meet: 'it's
the children's clothes and shoes. And when all the bills come in.
And the school trips and things.' One mother said it was 'difficult
especially in the holidays' and reckoned that she needed at least £10
extra 'when you have to pay for dinners, and they always want
money to spend.' Another said that she could not afford to go to the
shops 'so I get things out of catalogues so I can pay weekly... when
something big comes up like shoes or a coat it's hard to find a week
when I can afford it.' One summed it up: 'it's always difficult, the
whole time. You can't even buy decent food. Money's a big problem
when you're a single parent family.'

We explored issues to do with finances and health. Fifty eight of
the 125 households (46 per cent) contained an adult or child with
health problems. Forty-four households (35 per cent) contained
children with health problems, but this figure rose to 50 per cent for
lone parent households, compared with a third of the 'couple'
households. Adult health problems included anaemia, TB, epilepsy,
asthma, thalassaemia, anorexia nervosa, back injuries, kidney
conditions, diabetes, high blood pressure. Parents reported on
childhood complaints and allergies such as asthma, eczema, hay
fever, hearing difficulties, ear infections, infantile convulsions,
anaemia; other children had more serious conditions such as
thalassaemia, epilepsy, Down's Syndrome, deafness, or minor
deformities such as club foot. Others again had speech or learning
difficulties such as dyslexia.

Children's problems as well as adults' caused great distress
within the family, and were often the occasion of parents seeking
advice from the projects. One mother described her three year old's
asthma and convulsions in these words: 'he's very hard to handle—
it's hard to communicate with him, difficult to make him see what's

right and what's wrong; also he can hardly talk at all. He may end up in a special school.' Another described how her child suffered from what was now thought to be mild epilepsy: 'he was having epileptic fits from two and a half years—they knew there was something wrong but they didn't know what it was.' A third spoke of her child's 'behaviour difficulties: stomach aches and health problems—so they took us to the doctors... and put me in touch with a counselling service—somewhere else to go when you're desperate.'

Mothers described themselves as suffering from depression. One mother who said she had suffered from postnatal depression 'for a year' used to 'lock herself in the bedroom' after seeking help with her child who was a 'difficult feeder': 'he was very funny with his feeding... they give you all sorts of books and pamphlets... they could give me so much advice in the clinic but it wasn't as if I could come to a group—discuss it with somebody who was qualified in that field... behaviour patterns of children... if what he was doing was right for his age or if it was something we would have to put right...' Another mother with a young baby with breathing difficulties said, 'With a first child and no children in the family you don't know much; you have a child, and you come home, and that's it—you could do what you like—bang them against a wall or whatever or you can get very depressed. Nobody bothers to find out; nobody bothers to keep an eye out.'

Financial difficulties (whether adults or children—the percentages here were the same, give or take a few points) certainly seemd to exacerbate health problems. 80 per cent of the households with health problems said they were in financial difficulties, compared with 69 per cent of 'healthy' households. Again, the picture was rather worse for lone parent households. 93 per cent of the lone parents with children with health problems were in financial difficulties, compared with 71 per cent of the 'couple' households. Thus only 6 per cent of the lone parents with children with health problems were *not* in financial difficulties, compared with 29 per cent of the 'couple' households. In other words, nine out of ten lone parents with children with a health problem had financial difficulties—and even seven out of ten couple parents in this position had financial difficulties as well.

Young families may be in a particularly vulnerable position as regards housing and geographical mobility. We hoped to estimate the effects of this on children by asking how many moves families had made within the last five years, and from how far afield. 28 per cent of our families had maintained their stability during this period and had not moved house at all. But many had moved around a good deal: one in five families (21 per cent) had made three or more moves. One in three families (34 per cent) had moved once, and slightly more than one in three (38 per cent) had moved twice. When we asked about the most recent move, 56 per cent had moved within the local area, 75 per cent within the local region, and 25 per cent from further afield.

Two points should be made in summary so far. The first concerns children's experiences. We did not interview children directly, but their parents' accounts show clearly that a considerable number of young children in this study were growing up in disadvantaged circumstances. One child in four was growing up with a lone parent, many of whom were dependent on benefits and in financial difficulties. Children in forty-five of the 125 households were growing up dependent on benefits. Forty-four households (sixteen headed by lone parents) had children with health problems; thirty-five of these households (fifteen headed by lone parents) also had financial difficulties. Children in forty-four families had moved twice or more in the last five years, and in twenty-four families they had moved three times or more, with the loss of friends and familiar surroundings particularly disruptive for those under five.

The second point concerns the measurement of disadvantage. The data described so far on household type, health, income and stability in the area provide some measures of comparison of a rough and ready kind between the six areas. It is clear that many families suffered from multiple disadvantages. But it is impossible to estimate whether this group of family centre clients as a whole was more or less disadvantaged than groups using other forms of preschool provision in the six areas or indeed non-users, because no comparative data was collected of this kind. However, it should be possible to make some comparison of levels of disadvantage between this group and households with dependent children in general in the six areas when the data from the 1991 census become available.

One comparison of a very limited kind can be made between referred and non-referred users. When we interviewed families, although we did not ask directly, it quickly became apparent when they or their children had been referred by the statutory services to the project—for example, when respondents were asked how they had first heard of the centre and the purpose for which they had first attended. This data is limited in value by very small numbers, and by the fact that the term 'referral' clearly had a different significance in different centres. Preliminary analysis of users at one centre, where half the users had been referred by social workers or health professionals and half were local 'open access' users, shows that the referred group contained more lone parent households, with slightly more financial difficulties, dependence on benefits rather than wages, and health problems. This is consistent with the picture from the rest of the study. That 'referred' families are often unhealthy and in financial need is not surprising; the surprise is that 'open access' families run them so close.

Bringing up Young Children in the Six Areas

What sort of picture of the six local areas did respondents paint? We wanted to know what life was like for parents (mainly mothers in this study) bringing up a young family. What were the community and family networks? Did the mothers in our study get enough support in their daily lives from their friends, neighbours, and communities, and enough opportunities to develop their own interests and capabilities? What part did the family centres play?

Parents' levels of satisfaction or dissatisfaction with neighbourhood or housing provide important clues to children's experience. Opinion was divided. 42 per cent thought their neighbourhood was not a good environment in which to bring up small children. Parents spoke of small rooms, overcrowding, poor heating, lack of outside playspace. Many also criticised their neighbourhoods for unsafe roads and dangerous traffic, pollution, noise, litter, dangerous play equipment, dogs, drugs, abusive adults or rough older children, and, sometimes, hostile neighbours. 'It's racist, violent, mucky—not a good place at all.' 'It can be a bit bad round here with racism.' 'There's too much traffic—dogs get into the garden—children can get out at the front—muck from the works gets into the garden as well.' 'I don't like it round here—all the break-ins and rapes and people mucking about with kids—taking them away and that. Like at the school they've had some man showing himself to the kids. But I suppose it happens everywhere.' 'You've got a great big road down the middle of our street—she's nearly got killed. Vindictive neighbours—there's always trouble at your door. People know you come here (to the family centre)—they threaten me—and the kids—kick your door in, kick the fence down...'. 'It's not very friendly. They turn their back on you. They hate you because they think you hit your kids...'. 'Too many bad people... too much crime round here. It's not safe to let (the child) out unsupervised— other kids are violent.'

However, 41 per cent thought their neighbourhoods were reasonable environments for bringing up young children, or at least better than their previous circumstances. As one woman said, it was great to have a council house of your own after living in bedsits and moving around a lot. Some of the centres served several different neighbourhoods, and users had mixed views: 'This end of the estate is fine—the other end is a lot of trouble. We've had a couple of stabbings. I wouldn't let him go out on his own. It's too closed in— all trees—you can't see the road from the pathways. But there are a lot of kids for him to play with.'

We asked parents to consider a list of twelve items which we introduced as 'some of the things people say are important when bringing up under fives' (Table 1). What stood out in this list?

Table 1
What do you think is important in bringing up young children?
(N = 125)

	Yes	No	Number of respondents
'Somewhere to go for child to be with other children'	94%	6%	(113)
Other adults to talk to	94%	6%	(115)
Money to spend on children	90%	10%	(115)
Playspace for children	89%	11%	(114)
Friends and relatives for advice	83.5%	16.5%	(115)
Time off	80%	12%	(125)
Nurseries for working parents	72%	28%	(116)
Baby-sitting	72%	28%	(112)
Transport	72%	28%	(112)
Experts for advice	70%	30%	(115)
Help with shopping	48%	52%	(115)
Help at difficult times (eg bedtimes)	30%	70%	(113)

Parents' needs for social contact ('other adults to talk to') and children's need for social experience ('somewhere to go for children to be with other children') came tied top, with 94 per cent of the parents agreeing that these were important. Next came money to spend on the children, with 90 per cent saying this was important—not surprisingly, given the high levels of financial difficulties found in this sample of families. Playspace for children came next, with 89 per cent agreeing this was important—again not surprising, given the comments on dangerous or violent neighbourhoods and the need for safety and supervision. Support networks ('having friends and relatives to go to for advice') came next, with 83 per cent rating this as important—although some parents said they would not necessarily go to relatives for this sort of support, and others said it was not always advice they needed—more a 'listening ear' or 'a chance to let your hair down' or practical help like looking after the child for a short time.

'Time off' ('having time away from the children and time for yourself') was rated as important by 80 per cent. Day care and baby-sitting were rated as important by 72 per cent, and so was transport. Expert advice was thought to be important by 70 per cent, although there were some argument about the term—some parents saying they would go to a named person (usually a health visitor or a member of staff in the family centre) or their own mother 'rather than an expert', while others said 'we're all experts'.

Here are some examples of parents' replies when we asked them what was important when bringing up a young family. 'Money for food and bills.' 'Your mum's support.' 'If I didn't have my parents to baby-sit I'd just stay in—I wouldn't leave them with anyone else.' 'Knowing what they (the children) need to do before they've got to go to school.' 'Helping me to learn how to cope, especially with (the child's) behaviour problems. How does a normal five-year-old behave?' 'Somebody to say to me when I'm getting frustrated... thinking I've got problems—to say, look, you're doing OK—moral support—knowing I've got somebody who knows what it's like.' 'I'd like to be able to talk more to the health visitors or doctors, but they are always too busy.'

'I was having problems at home, and coping with the children... problems with myself... mainly to do with my son... I had the problem of... my daughter burning herself as well—and it wasn't through my fault... you see this was before they recognised that she had a hearing problem. So what everything I said "no" she just done the opposite and went and done things... I don't get depressed, it's the anger...'.

Table 2
Bringing up young children. Do you get *enough* of this sort of help?
(N = 125)

	Yes	No	Number of respondents
Friends and relatives for advice	84%	16%	(93)
Experts for advice	81%	19%	(79)
Other adults to talk to	80%	20%	(105)
'Somewhere to go for child to be with other children'	78%	22%	(100)
Help at bedtimes etc	77%	23%	(44)
Help with shopping	74%	26%	(53)
Playspace for children	73.5%	26.5%	(98)
Baby-sitting	62%	38%	(81)
Transport	57%	43%	(89)
Money to spend on children	47.5%	52.5%	(101)
Time off	45%	55%	(100)
Nurseries for working parents	27%	73%	(67)

(In order—ie only 27% parents (67 respondents) thought that they had enough childcare for working parents; while 84% (93 respondents) thought they had enough advice from friends and relatives.)

'Your husband—he's got to understand. (Having a baby is) such a change in your life. (Support from) your mother—and also your friends—my friend got me out of my depression—she made me get dressed and go out. You need someone like a health visitor or a midwife. My depression lasted three months—depression and isolation—it's amazing how it can change your personality. My friends stopped coming round, and my husband's friends wouldn't come round—you know, "what's the matter with her, then?"'

We then asked parents if they got enough help with what they had identified as important. Some clear patterns began to emerge (Table 2).

Eight out of ten parents thought they had enough support from friends and relatives (84 per cent), enough expert advice (81 per cent), and enough adult contact (80 per cent). Seven out of ten thought they had enough access to playspace (73 per cent) and socialising (78 per cent) for their children. On the other hand, more than half the parents thought they did not get enough time to themselves away from their children (55 per cent), enough money to spend on their children (52 per cent), or day care (73 per cent).

Finally we asked whether the family centre had made any difference. Again some clear patterns began to emerge (Table 3). The projects' clearest contribution was to opportunities for children: nine out of ten parents (93%) thought the projects had helped with providing opportunities for children's social development—

Table 3
Bringing up young children. Has the Family Centre made any difference?
(N = 125)

	Yes	No	Number of respondents
'Somewhere to go for child to be with other children'	93%	7%	(70)
Playspace for children	81%	19%	(68)
Time off	72%	28%	(65)
Other adults to talk to	66%	34%	(74)
Experts for advice	49%	51%	(45)
Help with shopping	35%	65%	(23)
Nurseries for working parents	30%	70%	(37)
Transport	29.5%	70.5%	(44)
Friends and relatives for advice	28%	72%	(53)
Baby-sitting	11%	89%	(47)
Money to spend on children	11%	89%	(35)
Help at bedtimes etc	5%	95%	(19)

'learning to mix', 'learning to share', 'he's not so spiteful'—and eight out of ten (81 per cent) thought the projects had helped with safe playspace. Seven out of ten parents (72 per cent) thought that the projects had given them time off—'you can leave him there while you do a bit of shopping'. There was also a very positive view of opportunities to share problems and experiences with other parents: 66 per cent thought the projects had helped with 'having other adults to talk to'—'you find you're not on your own', 'I've made some good friends', 'you don't feel so isolated' were frequent comments.

The largest discrepancies were to do with financial help and day care. Nine out of ten parents had identified money to spend on the children as important, but only four out of ten thought they had sufficient, and only one in four thought the projects helped financially. Perhaps this is not surprising given the level of financial need evident in ths survey, but it should perhaps lead us to ask about the projects' involvement in money advice or income support work, or practical support for job generation schemes or credit unions, and publicity for services that were available. Seven out of ten parents thought that day care was important, but only two out of ten thought there was enough help with this and only three out of ten thought the projects were any help. Again, this level of demand is not surprising given national trends, but it is clear that the family centres did not give day care a high priority.

Here are some examples of parents' comments about the impact of the family centres for them and their children.

'I've made some friends through the centre—and it's changed my child. I was so protective, it was terrible—I'd panic if I couldn't see him. But it's better since I've been coming to the centre, I'm not as bad as I used to be.'

'I couldn't imagine not coming now. (It's) actually working on my problems... It gives you time for yourself and space that you need. You're classed as special and very important. At first I resented it, but now—you're somebody—not just an object beneath your problems...'.

'It's calmed me down a bit, I think. It's made me look at things a bit more in perspective instead of getting so wound up... over things... More confidence... it's made me look at my future... maybe going to college and things like that which I probably never would have thought about before... (My son's) been such a difficult person it's very hard to leave him with anybody really, so I never really got any time on my own at all. The only people I could leave him with was my mum... and my friend up the road... So down there (at the centre) at least I knew that he was learning as well as being looked after which I appreciated very much.'

'We used to have a regular (baby-sitter) but not recently. It's difficult to get someone genuine and reliable... There's no baby-sitting circle (where I live)—socialising is a problem. The family centre is the only access I have to other adults because I don't have many friends (on my estate).'

'It changed my life. It helped me to be more patient with my children and to be. . . more assertive—to go for things you wouldn't dream of doing before. . . I used to be shouting at my child a lot—lost my temper and I just used to scream with frustration—I've learned patience—it's made me see it's not just *my* children.'

And for their children: 'she used to be dead whingy—all she used to do was sit and moan and whinge—now she'll draw if she's bored like the other kids do—and she's learnt to share through having other kids to play with.'

Themes from the Research: Discussion and Conclusions

This preliminary analysis makes three points. First, the importance of play and socialising for young children, and secondly the importance of social support for parents. While nine out of ten parents in the sample thought that safe playspace and opportunities for children to learn to share and become independent were important, only four out of ten thought that the projects were aiming to provide a centre where parents with young children could meet or where young children could play. But half the sample thought that the projects' main focus was on the children, and nearly six out of ten thought that the centres had in fact helped their child to learn to mix. Eight out of ten parents thought the centres had helped them as parents to make friends. For parents, these were the two most important aspects of the projects.

The third aspect is the level of need revealed by the study. Although the small referred group contained more lone parent households and had more health and financial problems, the level of difference between referred and non-referred was small. The more important point is that levels of need were also very high in the non-referred group.

This was a small study, and not based on a random sample of centres, so we should not generalise from the conclusions. Our preliminary analysis shows that on some measures these centres were clearly successful. They were attracting a range of families with high levels of need, which must be one measure of effectiveness. 97 per cent of this sample said they would recommend the centre to someone else, and many had already done so—an indication of consumer satisfaction. And the interviews provided some vivid examples of commendation. However, further analysis is needed of users' criticisms, differences between 'referred' and 'non-referred' users, the 'fit' between professional and user views, and different aspects of user participation in the centres.

This study was framed in the tradition of consumer research which treats users' views not just as symptoms but as valid descriptions in their own right. It is therefore proper to investigate users' definitions of need and to scrutinise whether professionals' and users' views match or not. The view presented of bringing up young children indicates a broad range of needs not restricted to the referred minority in this study. This finding is consistent with a broad rather than a narrow interpretation of 'children in need' and thus has obvious implications for implementation of the Children Act. It is also relevant for the notion of 'partnership', which requires a clear understanding of users' views and judgements as well as those of professionals.

References

Calam, R. and Franchi, C. (1987): *Child abuse and its consequences: observational approaches.* Cambridge: Cambridge University Press.

Cigno, K. (1988): 'Consumer views of a family centre drop-in.' *British Journal of Social Work.* 18, 361-375.

Daines, R. Lyon, K. and Parsloe, P. (1990): *Aiming for partnership.* Barkingside: Barnardo's.

De'Ath, E. (1988): *The family centre approach.* Focus on families (No 2). Briefing Paper. London: Children's Society.

Department of Health (1991): *The Children Act 1989 guidance and regulations: volume 2 family support, day care and educational provision for young children.* London: HMSO.

Ferri, E. and Saunders, A. (1991): *Parents, professionals and pre-school centres: a study of Barnardo's provision.* London: National Children's Bureau.

Gibbons, J. (1990): *Family support and prevention: studies in local areas: purposes and organisation of preventive work with families.* London: HMSO.

Holman, B. (1988): *Putting families first: prevention and child care.* Basingstoke: Macmillan.

CHAPTER 2

Provision of Support Through Family Projects

Jane Gibbons

Introduction

Many people believe that prevention is better than cure, but it has not proved easy to demonstrate the success of preventive services in reducing needs for care, or in reducing the incidence of serious child rearing problems. Confusion partly arose from the multiple and diverse objectives that preventive services were supposed to fulfil. The Children Act (1989) has made local authorities' responsibilities clearer: on the one hand there is the duty to provide family support services to children in need and their families, with no *specific* preventive intention. On the other hand there remains a duty to provide services specifically aimed at preventing entry into long-term care or court proceedings. In this chapter I shall be concerned with family support provision under the first heading—that is, without a *specific* preventive intention. The chapter will describe an approach in one local authority that concentrated on strengthening family support resources in local neighbourhoods that contained many poor families with young children and were high on measures of social need. This approach can be linked with ideas about primary prevention.

In public health, primary prevention refers to measures which prevent illness from developing—for example, vaccination against smallpox. Secondary prevention involves early diagnosis of cases of illness—for example through screening instruments—in order to intervene at the earliest possible stage. Roy Parker (1980) applied this framework to children's services, drawing a distinction between 'primary' (universal) services which reduce the general levels of poverty and insecurity, and 'secondary' services restricted to those identified as at special risk.

However, it may be a forlorn hope to attempt to identify *in advance* families where serious child rearing problems are going to occur. All the evidence is that, although it may be possible to pick out a majority of those who go on to harm their children, this is always at the price of wrongly identifying a much larger number of false positives—parents with similar characteristics who never harm their children. Therefore, in child and family social work, it is probably better to combine a strategy of primary prevention with one of adequate intervention as soon as possible *after* the event.

Family Support Strategy

By definition, primary preventive measures are not targeted on individual families identified as at risk. But they could be targeted on particular neighbourhoods, where there are many sources of stress and few compensating assets. Indeed there is some evidence that it is just this sort of neighbourhood that produces high rates of serious child rearing problems and entry to care (Garbarino & Gillam, 1980; Cotterill, 1988). It is argued that family support provisions would have most effect if they were concentrated in areas of high stress and low personal and material resources, containing many young families. Supportive provisions in these areas would not be aimed at families with identified problems, but would be open to all families. Family centres might serve as a focus for this sort of provision.

Under the Children Act local authorities are required to facilitate the provision by others (including in particular voluntary organisations) of services which they themselves have power to provide. The Act goes further than before in stressing partnership between local authority and voluntary providers and in this respect it can be seen as consistent with the philosophy underlying the Community Care reforms.

In the research project on which this chapter is based (Gibbons et al., 1990) we were interested in a strategy for the development of family support provision, whereby local authorities would fulfil their duty to promote the welfare of children in need largely indirectly, through supporting a variety of independently-run voluntary or informal neighbourhood groups. If these family projects were to benefit the clients of social services departments, social workers in those departments would need to become skilled at linking individual children and families in need with services outside the direct control of their own department. Local authority financial support of independent family projects could be more easily justified if it could be demonstrated that they were being used by families with many needs, as well as by other families, that families benefited, and that family projects could actually 'divert' some families seeking certain kinds of support away from the social services department.

Social Support as a Buffer Against Stress

Under the Children Act, 'family support' is defined in terms of services provided to meet needs. This is a far better approach than one which defined need for support in terms of various parental deficiencies, but it does seem possibly to underplay the importance of less tangible kinds of support.

In the health field, there is a large body of research into the role of social support in mitigating the effects of stress. People need 'supplies' (emotional and cognitive as well as practical) from each other in order to maintain equilibrium. Adequate social support may have a direct effect on individuals' mental or physical health, so that people lacking support are more likely to develop illness. Or social support may act as a 'buffer'', warding off the worst effects of stress so that those with adequate support are more likely to weather adverse life events. One of the most powerful kinds of social support in its effects has been shown to be the availability of a close, confiding relationship with another person. It is reasonable to suppose, then, that families in need who are linked with sources of support in the community will be more able to overcome difficulties than families lacking such support.

The Family Support Research

We studied the organisation of family support provision in two contrasting areas—Oldweigh and Newpath, both urban areas in mainly rural counties. Demographically the areas were very similar. They differed in their policies towards children and families and, in particular, in their approach to partnership with the voluntary sector.

In Newpath during the 1980s seven new family projects had been developed, six of them on housing estates with many social needs.

Table 1
The Family Projects

Project	Year	Funders	Neighbourhood Base	1988 Budget
Herding	1981	Children's Society + County Council	Yes	29,000
Home-Start	1982	Health (Jnt. Finance)	No	37,380
Newton	1983	Nat. Children's Home + County Council	Yes	52,000
Hildon	1983	Urban Aid	Yes	21,000
Acorn	1984	Children's Society + Health (Jt. Fin.)	Yes	40,000
Ashgrove	1985	Urban Aid	Yes	54,000
Meadow	1988	NSPCC + County Council	Yes	NK

The research was intended to document how this provision had been built up and maintained, how the projects were managed and staffed, the services they offered to the local communities and how they were used. The other main purpose of the research was to examine the effect of the projects on the work of the social services department, the links established between statutory and voluntary family support provision and the nature of their partnership. Three linked surveys of families with children under 14 were undertaken:

1. A randomly selected sample of parents living in Newpath in the areas surrounding the new family projects (the community sample).

2. A sample of parents from the same areas who were referred to Newpath social services.

3. A sample of parents referred to social services in the comparison area of Oldweigh.

Through these surveys, we explored how parents saw their needs and problems, where they turned for help, and how social workers responded to requests for help.

We expected to find differences between Newpath, where there was a network of neighbourhood family projects as well as a generally vibrant voluntary sector, and Oldweigh, where there was less community development. We expected that:

• In Newpath, families in need of straightforward advice services would be diverted away from social services to the new family projects and that consequently referrals to social services in Newpath would contain a higher proportion of families with serious child-rearing problems;

• In Newpath, social workers would demonstrate more knowledge and use of community resources;

• Families in Newpath would more often be linked to voluntary family support resources as a result of referral to social services;

• Families in Newpath would have better outcomes four months after referral.

Needs and Problems of Referred and Community Parents

The families referred to social services in both Newpath and Oldweigh differed markedly from other local families. They were more often headed by a lone parent (usually a divorced woman).

They endured more poverty and housing problems. They differed in their attitudes to housing and neighbourhood: they more often wanted to move, less often felt the neighbourhood was a good one in which to bring up children and less often described the neighbourhood as friendly.

Family problems perceived by parents were measured by their answers to questions in a Family Problem Questionnaire and in the Malaise Inventory. The first provided scores for problems concerned with lack of social contact; parent-child relationships; ill-health; finances; and marital relations. The second contained 24 questions about emotional distress, with a cut-off score of seven conventionally serving as a marker for clinical anxiety and depression. There were marked differences between the parents referred to social services and the community sample (Table 2).

Table 2
Family Problems: Differences between Referred and Community Parents

Problem Types	Referred (143)	Community (359)
	% 3+ serious problems	
Finances	67	13
Social Contact	56	17
Parent-Child	43	8
Marital	39	12
Health	23	5
Malaise Score 7 +	59	21

In summary, a referred parent was more likely to be coping alone, to have financial and housing problems, to be lonely, anxious and depressed and to be burdened by a range of non-financial family problems to do with relationships and health. Money problems, lack of social contacts and loneliness were the problems most often mentioned by parents themselves. Family support services should be addressing these needs.

Use of Support

Informal Support
All the parents who took part in the research were asked a series of questions in order to identify the people to whom they turned for different kinds of help and support. 'Support' was classified as *instrumental* (practical help with childcare, loans etc); *emotional* (confiding private thoughts or feelings, getting praise or thanks or

advice); *social* (having a good time in company). Supporters were classified as relatives; friends; neighbours; other non-professionals; and paid professionals. Contrary to our expectation, referred and community parents identified similar numbers of instrumental, emotional and social supporters. But although the number of supporters was much the same there were differences in the quality of the support, from the parents' point of view. Referred parents' networks contained a significantly higher proportion of people with whom they expected to have an unpleasant interaction—an upset of some kind. In other words, these parents were experiencing others more often as sources of conflict and pain. Referred parents not surprisingly expressed significantly more needs for support, but less satisfaction with the support available to them (Table 3).

Table 3
Needs for and Satisfaction with Support: Community and Referred Parents

Support	Community	Referred
Needs Index	0.8(1.4)	2.6(3.5)***
Satisfaction Index	6.0(5.7)	4.1(3.7)***

*** One way analysis of variance p<.001
    Lone parents' index score in brackets

Organised Support

All the parents in the community survey were asked which community support services they had used in the past year, and how satisfied they were. Results are shown in Table 4.

Table 4
Parents' Use of Family Support Services

	Used Last Year	Very Satisfied
	%	%
Play Group	42	70
Health Visitor	47	64
C.A.B.	13	63
G.P.	94	62
Nursery School	12	60
Vol. Family Project	12	49
Police	23	46
Social Services	12	35
Social Security	33	25

BASE NUMBER = 359

Community health services were by far the most often used and most of their users were very satisfied. Play groups, the Citizens Advice Bureau and nursery schools were also rated very satisfactory by the majority of their users. Almost half those who had contacted one of the new family projects set up in Newpath were very satisfied. Users of the social services department and social security were rather less satisfied.

Users of the Family Projects

Through the Newpath community survey of 359 families living in the local areas served by the family projects, we tried to establish how well the projects were known, how widely they were used by the local population, and whether they were attracting families with many needs as well as more 'ordinary' families. Over 40 per cent had heard of one or more of the projects but a much smaller proportion had actually made contact with one. One reason was that many had only a vague idea of what the projects were for. Another reason was distance. But a common reason for avoiding the projects was that people perceived them as being for a certain kind of family—a problem family, or one that could not cope with its own difficulties. They did not wish to see themselves or their own families in this light. This may explain why three of the four neighbourhood projects had been used by only some ten per cent of respondents from their own local areas in the previous twelve months.

The neighbourhood projects were highly successful in reaching the families in the community with the greatest needs. In their own areas they were attracting more than a quarter of the poorest families. By contrast, only 4 per cent of low-need couples had ever contacted a family project. It is notable that, with the exception of Social Security, other community services did not attract higher proportions of disadvantaged families. Playgroups, for example, attracted 71 per cent of families of under-fives with *least* social disadvantages compared to 46 per cent of the most socially disadvantaged.

In spite of the variability in the expectations and experiences of people who contacted the projects, some patterns could be discerned. There seemed to be three typical patterns of use. **Consumers** did not see themselves as in need of help, but wanted to take advantage of a facility on offer at a project. They did not (or had not at the time of interview) progressed on from this to any wider involvement in the organisation of the project itself.

> They have a thrift shop where you can buy second-hand clothes. I don't go there for any other reason.

I just go to the Mother and Toddler group to meet friends, that's all.

Clients were using a project—in rather the same way that they might have used a solicitor or social services—because they needed help. They obtained some service—whether counselling, advisory or practical—and were apparently content with the role of service recipient, not seeking any wider involvement.

> I phoned up for an appointment and saw someone who gave me advice. That's all I wanted—advice about financial matters.

> I just needed someone to listen to me, just someone to talk to when I was feeling down. I didn't join in anything else, just had someone to visit me.

The final group may be called **members** of a project. These were people who may have started out as 'consumers' or 'clients' but whose involvement with the project had taken on a broader character. They had become identified with it, to the point where they were prepared to play a more active part in its running. They now saw themselves as helping others as well as being helped by their involvement. **Members** took part in a wider range of project activities than the other two user groups. They reported more benefits to themselves from their contact with a project (Table 5).

Table 5
What Users Gained from Attending Family Projects

Outcome	Consumers	Clients	Members
		% with outcome	
Had a good time	57	23	100
Made new friends	36	23	88
Gained confidence	21	23	75
Had help with children	14	23	62
Helped others	14	23	88
Understood self better	0	31	62
Understood others better	7	31	75
Learned something new	7	15	75
Spoke up in meetings	7	0	50
Helped to run activities	0	0	100
Took part in decisions	0	0	62
Took on new responsibilities	7	0	50
BASE	14	13	8

Overall the most commonly experienced gains were in increased opportunities for social contact and having a good time. These positive social outcomes should not be underestimated on estates where, as we have seen, loneliness and isolation were commonly experienced. By enlarging parents' social circles in this way, the family projects may be helping to increase their resilience and ability to cope with stress. The family projects were able to attract parents with the greatest level of need and all their users reported some gains. Those who became most engaged, and took on responsibilities within the project, reported most benefit.

The Social Services Department and Family Projects
What were the effects on social work practice in Newpath of having these new sources of family support in local communities? We had predicted a number of differences between Oldweigh and Newpath that would reflect the different family support resources available in the two areas.

However, there was no evidence for our view that the pattern of referrals would differ (because parents in need of money advice or practical help would be diverted to local family projects). Just as many people in Newpath as in Oldweigh came to social services solely for this kind of help, in spite of the fact that they would have got a better welfare rights service in several of the family projects.

There was also no evidence that Newpath social workers differed in knowledge of or attitudes to voluntary provision. They were no more often in contact with volunteers or voluntary groups, and their attitudes to preventive work in general were only slightly more favourable (Table 6).

Table 6
Social Workers' Attitudes to Preventive Work in Oldweigh and Newpath

	Oldweigh (35)	Newpath (31)
	% Agreeing	
Shortage of resources makes it very difficult to undertake non-statutory work	86	74
Preventive social work is a luxury not a priority for social services staff	57	38
There need to be big changes in our organisation so that our team can spend more time in preventive work	91	83
I would like to do preventive work but I don't have time	77	67

Parents referred to social services in Newpath were no more likely than those in Oldweigh to be linked to voluntary resources as a *result* of referral. As predicted, families in Newpath were in contact with more voluntary agencies and groups. But there was no evidence that social workers in Newpath, any more than those in Oldweigh, had made the links between families and voluntary sources of support. Families were in contact with a mean 1.12 voluntary resources before referral, and only 1.08 afterwards.

Thus, although the new family projects could not have been established without the political and financial support of the social services department, no policies had been developed which might have brought about a change in the roles of social services staff to take full advantage of them. One of the reasons for this was the siege mentality that had grown up in response to the growing number of child abuse referrals, and the shift of resources into investigating and managing case conferences. This had led, for example, to the abandonment of plans to 'outpost' social workers to the new family centres.

However, our prediction that referred parents' problems would show more improvement in Newpath than in Oldweigh was supported. After four months, Newpath parents showed more improvement in social contact, parent-child difficulties, finances and malaise: there were statistically significant differences between Oldweigh and Newpath parents four months after referral in levels of social contact and malaise. 61 per cent of Newpath parents said their problems were 'better' in comparison to 42 per cent of Oldweigh parents; more were satisfied or very satisfied with the help received. In other words, there was consistent evidence from the various measures of outcome that the referred families in Newpath appeared to be coping with their problems more successfully than those in Oldweigh. The most likely reason appeared to be differences in informal supportive networks and in contact with community resources, in particular day care.

The research provided some reasons to think that parents under stress more easily overcome family problems when there are many sources of family support available in local communities. The most useful form of provision may be good quality day care. However, it is not enough just to create the provision. Equal attention has to be paid to methods of linking vulnerable families into it.

References
Cotterill, A. M. (1988) The geographic distribution of child abuse in an inner-city borough. *Child Abuse & Neglect* **12**, 461-467.

Garbarino, J. and Gillam G. (1980) *Understanding Abusive Families* Lexington: Lexington.

Gibbons, J., Thorpe, S. and Wilkinson, P. (1990) *Family Support & Prevention: Studies in Local Areas* London: HMSO.

Parker, R. A. ed. (1980) *Caring for Separated Children: Plans, Procedures and Priorities* London: Macmillan.

PART 2

Studies of Selective Provision

CHAPTER 3

NEWPIN: a Befriending Scheme and Therapeutic Network for Carers of Young Children

Antony Cox, Andrea Pound and Christine Puckering

Introduction by Andrea Pound

NEWPIN is a befriending scheme and therapeutic network for families with young children. It was founded in 1980 in Walworth, a particularly deprived area of South London, as a result of concern by local professionals at the high levels of child abuse and family distress in the area. Ann Jenkins, a local health visitor and now a Group Analyst and Director of National NEWPIN, was appointed as the first co-ordinator. NEWPIN was located in an old health centre, and provided a large and welcoming living room, a well equipped creche, a kitchen, office and outside play-space. NEWPIN now has four centres in London, and more are being developed around the country. In its reliance on volunteer support and its overall aims it has some aspects in common with Homestart, a home visiting and befriending scheme which now has a 100 or so projects around the country, but NEWPIN has developed over time a more intensive therapeutic orientation.

The Structure of NEWPIN

Referrals are received mainly from health visitors and social workers and depression, isolation and problems in parenting are the most common problems at referral. NEWPIN has a particular remit for the prevention of child abuse, for which it won the Henry Kempe award in 1989. Its clients include a high proportion of women with long-standing mental health problems, women abused as children and families living in exceptionally adverse circumstances. Referrals to NEWPIN are first assessed at home for suitability for its approach, with a 'focus for change' being agreed in most cases towards the end of the interview. This may perhaps concern a mother's depression, anxiety, the relationships with children or partners, or her self-image and self-development. Depending on the nature of the problem, she may then be offered a befriender to visit and support her at home, attendance at the Drop-In at the NEWPIN centre, a therapeutic group, individual counselling, or several of these options. The Drop-In, or NEWPIN living room is a source of support and companionship to all NEWPIN members, and is the focus of its ethos of mutual helping. Women who are severely depressed or having major problems in parenting and need a safe place may attend every day. In addition to home visiting and the Drop-In, every member also has a list of everyone else's telephone number, including the staff, and can call on them at any time of the day or night, a privilege which has rarely, if ever, been abused. As we often heard in the research interviews 'in NEWPIN there is always someone there for you'. Art and writing workshops, visits to the country and many other constuctive activities are also generated by and for the membership and their children.

NEWPIN Training Programmes

Most members of NEWPIN sooner or later, depending on their circumstances, enter the befrienders' Training Programme, which now consists of a 32 week course running for two half days a week. One session consists of workshops and lectures on pregnancy and childbirth, child development, marriage, social issues affecting families, bereavement, loss and depression, approaches to child abuse, and the befriending relationship itself. The second session is devoted to a self-development group run by a group therapist in which members are encouraged to explore and come to some degree of reconciliation with past experience and particularly relationships with parent-figures. Following training, befrienders are attached to recently referred women, and continue to attend a regular supervision group.

Some experienced befrienders then go on to the two-year Co-ordinators Training Programme, which consists of lectures and workshops, attendance at an introductory counselling course and in-service training at an established NEWPIN centre. Many other members go on to take further education courses or go into paid work, and there is often a remarkable flowering of talent in women who have become deeply engaged in NEWPIN.

The NEWPIN Philosophy

NEWPIN is aiming at fundamental personal change in parents and children, going well beyond containment and emotional support. Few services have exposed themselves to such searching research scrutiny as NEWPIN, but one advantage has been an unusual degree of insight into the process of change within its therapeutic milieu. Three major components of NEWPIN's working principles have emerged—namely acceptance, attachment and insight into patho-logical projective mechanisms, especially in relation to child abuse.

Acceptance

Each NEWPIN member is accepted as someone of value with all their short-comings, their despair, mistrust, anger, helplessness and violence—but they are also challenged, and there is a strong expectation of change and growth. The daily events of NEWPIN are used to question previously unquestioned beliefs—that you will always be a victim, that you have to fight for everything, that no one can be trusted, that you are too useless or bad for anyone to love or care for. By sharing their experiences women discover they are not alone. Shame and guilt diminish as a result of help given 'for real', not because someone is paid to do it, and by discovering they can help others in return.

Attachment

Many of NEWPIN's members have suffered from repeated loss of attachment figures in early life or have never experienced a stable attachment figure at any time. Many have also suffered from further rejection, loss and abuse in adult life. Testing out of the befriender is a common occurrence in the initial stages of engagement, with withdrawal and avoidance or ambivalent, stormy relationships resembling the patterns of insecure attachment in young children. The stability and security of relationships could therefore be seen as a major factor in NEWPIN's therapeutic effectiveness—'we are always here for each other', 'NEWPIN is there, the bond is always there'. This sounds remarkably close to how people would describe their 'good enough' families.

Insight into Pathological Mechanisms

The basic philosophy of unconditional regard and respect for all NEWPIN members extends to the abusive parent, who is seen as attacking the child because it is bad, as he or she was made to feel bad as a child. The more the self is hated and despised the more perfect the child has to be as evidence of some goodness in the parent. The dynamic of projective identification is powerful enough to overwhelm the desire felt by all but the most socio-pathic parents to care well for their children. It follows that only when the parent discovers that he or she is of value, and worthy of love and concern, will the child be freed from the burden of the parent's projection, become an individual in his own right and be safe from further attack. Meanwhile, NEWPIN provides more intensive surveillance and support than any but the most specialised agencies could achieve.

Conclusion

To conclude, NEWPIN is an important new development in services for vulnerable parents and children, providing intensive support without dependency and loss of self respect. Health and Local Authorities are now being encouraged by the requirements of the Children Act to contribute to a project which provides intensive support and therapy for families under stress, preventing child abuse and neglect and the reception of children into care.

Research Evaluation of NEWPIN:
Overview by Antony Cox

Introduction

The research had as its starting point the view that the core function of family support is to address the quality of family relationships. What follows is a brief description of our research evaluation of NEWPIN and what we learned from it. The methodology was systematic and used standardised approaches to assessment. It broke new ground because of the detailed evaluation of the quality of parent/child relationships as a crucial outcome measure. Figures to support what is reported here are available in the final report to the Department of Health (Cox et al., 1990).

The research team is made up of clinicians who, in addition to doing the research, work on a day to day basis with families similar to those attending NEWPIN. It has been suggested that hard-nosed research is not relevant to the evaluation of voluntary family support schemes nor even some professional ones. Children do not make these distinctions; their need is for relationships to improve. Last week I was involved with a nine year old living with a single parent—a mother who had had a schizophrenic illness that resulted in chronic lack of responsiveness to the child. When the nine year old was asked 'What's it like now?' she said 'It's a little better'. A two year old child cannot tell you even that much: you have to look at the relationship. That is what the research set out to do and I emphasise that it is important for family support, whether professional or voluntary. It is no good doing well-meaning things that do not meet children's needs.

Systematic Research Evaluation of NEWPIN

Following a pilot study the research group obtained a grant from the Department of Health for a substantive study to be carried out over two years. The aim was to examine changes in the mother/child relationship as well as changes in the mothers themselves.

Essentially the research design involved assessing mothers and children at two points in time, six months apart. There was a study group of 40 NEWPIN families and a comparison group of 26 from another inner London borough where a NEWPIN project was proposed but had not yet started. NEWPIN families were either already involved or had recently been referred. During the six-month period, half of the NEWPIN group engaged in the training scheme while half were being supported and had not entered the training programme. Assessments were done in the home by members of the research team and included extensive interviews with mothers and videotaping interactions during bath times and meal times. These assessments occurred at both points in time.

What emerged from this exercise? There were both encouraging findings and important lessons to be learned. Some of these lessons appear to be of considerable importance not only to NEWPIN and other volunteer schemes, but also to family centres and other projects aiming to improve the quality of family life of parents and young children. Some apects of what was learnt emerged from the more formal data, while other feedback was drawn from comments of individual mothers.

1. NEWPIN recruited and sustained work with mothers who were not only experiencing current advertisities but who, in most instances, had themselves had a very troubled childhood involving for example: separation from parents (40 per cent), placement in care (33 per cent) or physical or sexual abuse (35 per cent). Half had experienced more than two years of significant mental ill health, sometimes extending back into the teenage years or even childhood. At initial evaluation two-thirds were currently clinically depressed and half had discordant relationships with partners.

2. Mothers recruited to NEWPIN who had experienced or were experiencing considerable adversity were nevertheless able to undertake training in personal development and assisting others and, indeed, those who had experienced more adversity or mental ill-health were more likely to sustain their adversity in the scheme.

3. Inter-personal responsibility is very important in voluntary work. Some mothers, 30 per cent at the time of the study, did not sustain significant involvement with NEWPIN. This was a larger proportion than at some other periods in NEWPIN's history and, from the mothers' comments, there were two important factors. Firstly, there were occasions when the supervision of women who were befriending others was not

adequately sustained. Secondly, there was a period when some
newcomers felt that it was difficult to break into already
established groups within the organisation. Both occurred at a
time of change within the project when less core support was
available. Feedback from the research heightened NEWPIN's
awareness of these issues, which they have energetically
addressed.

4. The experience of NEWPIN had a striking effect on those
    mothers who were well-involved with it in comparison with
    other mothers. Almost without exception they described
    changes in themselves, particularly in the areas of self-esteem
    and control over their lives. These changes were associated with
    improvements in maternal mental state.

5. Significant improvements in the mental state of mothers
    occurred where there had been between seven and twelve
    months involvement. Those with longer involvement had
    already changed by the start of the study. Those with shorter
    involvement changed less, so that it seemed that more than six
    months involvement was necessary for this to effect
    improvements in mental state. There is therefore an important
    question of the time scale of interventions to support families.

6. This comment is also relevent to the time scale of the research
    which allowed for a much briefer period of follow-up than the
    research group originally proposed. This study and indeed
    others have brought home the manner in which the benefits of
    various interventions may not be appreciated till a later stage,
    indeed beyond the time that the contact with the project has
    formally ceased. The continued influence of NEWPIN is given
    concrete expression by the frequency with which mothers have
    returned to make contact at a later stage.

7. Changing parent/child relationships is difficult. Overall there
    were significant improvements in the mothers' ability to
    anticipate their children's needs. There were changes in other
    areas but they were not statistically significant. These broad
    findings concealed that, on the one hand, there were
    undoubtedly mother/child pairs who changed quite dramatically
    but, on the other, there were some, including a few who had
    been involved in the scheme well before the study period, who
    had made no improvement at the follow-up assessment.
    NEWPIN has developed and is developing further approaches to
    meet the needs of these particular families.

There were important limitations of the evaluation, not least that the time period over which it took place was far too short. But these limitations do not vitiate the main findings. NEWPIN shows the way in which women with young families struggling against considerable adversity in their current lives and with the burden of having experienced a troubled childhood can build their confidence and self esteem in a fashion that professionally run services may find harder to achieve. But if a voluntary organisation is to attemnpt to meet the needs of such children and their families there must be a core of inter-personal responsibility, it could be called professionalism, in the way that the project is conducted in order to sustain contact with those who may be less readily engaged. The big challenge is the improvement of parent/child relationships and here the importance of inter-personal responsibility comes in the ability to recognise where there is more difficulty in effecting change, so that new and more intensive approaches can be implemented. As has been indicated, NEWPIN has taken this issue to heart and is introducing new approaches based on the research to help those mothers and children whose unsatisfactory relationship patterns are more entrenched. One crucial aspect of this is the provision of simultaneous 'holding' and positive experiences for both parent and child while work on the parent/child relationship is continuing. A third of the NEWPIN learning and self-development programme is now devoted to parent/child relationships.

Evaluating Parenting Through Direct Observation
by Christine Puckering

Evaluating parenting by observing actual interaction is time consuming and, therefore, expensive. The NEWPIN study used a team of researchers who visited families at home, filmed them on two occasions, and then analysed the video films and dealt with the statistics. Video-ing interaction at home had the advantage of providing a permanent record of the interaction so that the reliability of the observers could be checked, and also the tapes analysed by observers who were kept blind as to the group status of the mother, that is whether NEWPIN volunteer, referral or control and whether this was a baseline or follow-up tape.

We chose to film mothers and children at mealtimes and bathtimes for three reasons. The first was to provide some degree of standardisation in spite of the varying ages of the children from birth to about five or six years of age. Secondly we wanted the situation to be as natural as possible, and since mealtimes and bathtimes are commonplace for children, we hoped to be able to catch their habitual behaviour. Thirdly, by choosing a time when mothers had a task to complete we would 'stress' the system because the mother had an agenda to get through, not just play or watch the child. The mealtime and bathtime agenda offered many opportunities for mother and child to negotiate their differing wishes.

Our data from the video tapes was analysed using pre-defined and rigorously defined codes representing dimensions of parenting, which were validated from previous studies, or of theoretical interest according to the existing literature.

The Dimensions of Parenting
1. **Anticipation.** The observer recorded whether the mother took anticipatory action before she tackled a task which she knew might be difficult. For example, in changing the baby's nappy, does she give him a rattle before she begins to undress him to keep the 'fun' end of him happy while she deals with the other end. Waiting until the baby cries and then distracting him, would not count as anticipation, as the mother needed to show that she had facilitated getting the task done by taking action before she started caretaking. Even with young children, mothers will say 'One, two, three ... whee ...' before and during lifting them into the bath, for example, so that by tone of voice they alert the baby to expect a change.

2. **Autonomy.** The observer coded every example where the mother allowed the child a degree of choice or independence and recognised his individuality. For example, a mother can ask 'Do you want jam or honey on your toast', a very simple indication that the child has wishes of his own. In expressing a dislike of something, did the mother allow the child to protest even though the circumstances did not change? For example, a mother might say 'I know you don't like your hair being washed but it has to be done so we'll just get it over with quickly' when the child protested at hair washing.

3. **Co-operation.** We know from research studies (Parpal and Maccoby, 1985) that mothers who co-operate with their children have children who are more co-operative with them. The observers recorded any instances of the mother seeking co-operation from the child in a way that included explanations, facilitations, or any praise and approval for getting it right. Conversely, when the child made a request, we recorded not only whether the mother complied, but, if she did not comply, whether she sweetened the pill for the child by giving an explanation, for example not eating a third biscuit because it was nearly lunchtime. The observers also recorded whether the

mother and child escalated from co-operation into conflict. We measured how much conflict there was as well as whether mothers picked trivial issues over which to stage battles. Each instance of conflict was also classified as to whether the mother handled it effectively and without undue negative tone or comment.

4. **Child Distress.** We recorded the time each child spent crying but also whether the mother had precipitated the distress by, for example, hostile criticism, and whether once the child cried the mother was nasty to him or her during distress.

5. **Warmth and Stimulation.** The observers recorded all incidents of positive or negative affect, but also whether the mother was able to offer the child explanations and elaborations targeted at what the child was doing, and particularly whether she could maintain a playful interaction while also completing the mealtime or bathtime agenda.

The coding system counted clearly defined behaviours, and high reliability was maintained by inter-rater reliability checks and the compilation of a very detailed manual giving definitions and examples of the use of codes. The codes were not based on simple mechanics, for example, on whether the mother lifted the child out of the bath or told him to get into it, but on the style of interaction; that is, did she do it pleasantly, with warning before-hand, and praise afterward. This coding of intention was a mechanism to get around the difference in parenting tasks with a six month old and six year old.

In looking at our measures over time, only anticipation stands out as showing an improvement in the NEWPIN group. What was clear was that while a number of women showed a dramatic improvement, a substantial number did not. There are two possible explanations for the lack of demonstrated change. One is that there may not have been any change, and the second that there was change but we failed to measure it. If we were measuring the wrong things, then we might not have demonstrated change even if change had taken place.

Two pieces of evidence led us to believe that our measures were not inappropriate. Firstly, when we submitted our measures to a principal components analysis, three coherent factors emerged. The first was a hostility dimension which includes hostility from the mother, the precipitation of distress and being nasty in conflict issues. The second was an involvement-anticipation factor, including a number of anticipation measures along with stimulation and good co-operation. The third, less powerful, was a coercion-control factor with both many child requests and many control bouts and bad handling of conflict by the mother. These three factors are not only internally coherent but also theoretically plausible as important child rearing attributes. Secondly, when we compared our observation measures with the Richman Child Behaviour Questionnaire (Richman and Graham, 1971), the anticipation measures predicted child behaviour problems, that is mothers who were effectively anticipating and pre-empting difficulties had children with fewer behaviour problems. Overall then, we have two very different pieces of evidence that our measures are coherent, and go along with an externally validated measure of child disturbance.

Two other possible reasons for failing to demonstrate change are the relatively short period of follow-up and the possibility that while mothers have themselves begun to feel better, their parenting will on the whole not change unless it is directly addressed by the intervention. It is, of course, obvious that with very seriously disadvantaged women six months may be too short a time to effect change, and is certainly too short a time over which to measure change. We do, however, think that parenting does need to be addressed directly.

Changing Parenting
The research group has now begun to develop and pilot a parenting package based on the dimensions of parenting. This package is being implemented at NEWPIN by Mrs. Maggie Mills in Professor Cox's Unit at Guy's Hospital, and at a Social Work Department Family Centre in Alloa, Scotland. The parenting package uses handouts to ask the mothers to reflect on their own feelings, behaviour and reaction, and their children's. Having introduced each dimension of parenting, the women devise their own 'homework' exercises to practise the tasks. Practising giving choices like 'Do you want jam or honey on your toast' may not appear to be attacking the very root of difficult relationships but, by making the ideas very concrete, we hope to get the women to understand abstract ideas. The handouts are made 'user friendly'. For example, the anticipation dimension is introduced by a handout titles 'Spotting trouble before trouble spots you'. The groups also use videotapes of the women at home with their children from which they themselves have chosen extracts good and bad which they want to talk about in the group. The women also bring their children to the centre and spend time making a snack or doing an activity with one of the workers there to model, prompt and reinforce good interaction. All this can only happen in an atmosphere of co-operation where the women, many of whom have severe parenting

problems including children on the Child Protection Register, are themselves nurtured and supported by concurrent psychotherapy. Anonymous feedback on the groups by the consumers has been very good. One fairly representative mother reported 'I now know that my children are people with feelings, and their bad behaviour and good is something I can change. I used to think Joe was just bad, now I know he's just wanting something'.

In conclusion, NEWPIN has been successful in keeping families together and in protecting children. Evaluating our work is very important, for if we do not we cannot test our successes and failures or improve the help we bring to children within their families. We are immensely grateful to NEWPIN for their courage in allowing us to evaluate their work in such detail, a process of scrutiny which can be far from comfortable at times. Finally we ourselves need to evaluate our parenting package just as NEWPIN allowed us to evaluate them, so that we can continue to translate research into practice and back again into research.

References

Cox, A. D., Puckering, C., Pound, A., Mills, M. and Owen, A. L. (1990) *The Evaluation of a Home Visiting and Befriending Scheme: NEWPIN*. Final Report to Department of Health.

Parpal. M. and Maccoby, E. E. (1985). Maternal responsiveness and subsequent child compliance. *Child Development*, 56, 1326-1334.

Richman, N. and Graham, P. (1971). A behaviour screening questionnaire for use with 3 year old children. *J. Child Psychol. & Psychiat.*, 12, 5-33.

CHAPTER 4

Partnership with Parents of Children in Need of Protection

June Thoburn and Ann Lewis

Introduction: Boundary Issues and the Legal Context

The Children Act and Guidance, (including the latest version of *Working Together* (DH 1991), which has been substantially revised following the Act), leave no doubt that children in need of protection and their families should be offered support services under Part III of the Children Act. Only when voluntary methods of helping are unable to provide adequate protection should the compulsory powers of Parts IV and V of the Act be invoked. From early reports of the months following implementation, it appears that local authorities are, indeed, responding to this requirement of the Act, and the numbers of emergency protection orders are considerably lower than the corresponding numbers of place of safety orders taken under previous legislation. Indeed, in some areas it appears that the only work undertaken under Part III of the Act is in respect of children in need of protection—a fettering of discretion which appears to be contrary to the principles of the Act, and the Guidance (DH, 1991, para. 2.4) which states that it would 'not be acceptable' for an authority to confine support services to children at risk of significant harm.

Working together under the Childen Act 1989 (DH 1991) uses actual or suspected significant harm or likely significant harm as the triggers for child protection procedures as well as investigations under Section 47 of the Act, and this terminology will therefore be used in this paper. There are important changes from previous practice which have implications for the boundary between work which is conducted under the provisions of Section 17, and that which is under the provisions of Section 47. A careful reading of *Working Together* and the guidance to the Act suggest that the intention is to ensure greater clarity about those circumstances when it will be appropriate to use child protection procedures. In the first place, the tighter definition implied by the use of **suspicion or actual significant harm or likely significant harm** as the threshold for child protection procedures will mean that children who have in the past been provided with a service because of child protection registration

will in future fall outside the criteria for registration, and come under
the general provisions of Section 17. Whilst many authorities had
already moved in the direction of not using child protection
conferences and registers if a multi-disciplinary plan is not necessary
in order to protect the child who had been abused, most researchers
in this field have found that children have been registered in
circumstances which will no longer be appropriate if the new
Guidance is followed, either because the requirements of the
significant harm threshold are not met, or because a multi-
disciplinary protection plan is not needed. Many of these will have
been registered under the 'grave concern' category—a category
which no longer appears in the official guidance.

The practice of some local authorities of using registration as the
trigger for the provision of services will cease. At present, some
social workers, (and even more so other professionals), and indeed
family members themselves sometimes argue in favour of
registration in order to ensure that either services, or multi-agency
co-operation, are made available, even though it would be possible
to work in exactly the same way, and perhaps even more effectively,
without the use of the register.

This point has been made at some length, because there is a
difference in the nature of partnership between social workers,
parents and children, if the work is being conducted as part of a
Section 47 investigation, or if it is being provided as Section 17
support. In particular, there are big differences in the respective
powers of the social worker and the family members. If partnership
is to be anything other than tokenism in cases where there is concern
about the child's safety, it is essential for family members to know
when they really *do* have a choice, and when the power to make
decisions lies elsewhere. We shall return to this point later in this
chapter, but emphasise here that social workers need to be clear
about whether they are working at the Section 17 threshold of 'in
need', or the Section 47 threshold of 'in need of protection' and to
share this information and its implications for partnership and
choice with family members.

Finally in this introduction, before proceeding to a discussion of
the nature of partnership in protection cases we emphasise the
importance of Section 27 and Schedule 2(i), (iii)—that the assessment
of need must be conducted in a co-ordinated way by the various
agencies, and that the local authority may request the help of other
authorities in exercising its functions under Part III of the Act. In
other words, multi-agency work is encouraged when children are 'in
need' and not only when they are 'in need of protection'. Thus, the
tighter guidance in *Working Together* should mean that a greater
proportion of multi-agency conferences involving family members
will take place under the provisions of Sections 17 and 27 so that
coherent plans for supporting families under stress can be put into

place without the additional stress, stigma, and indeed cost, of the higher level and more expensive child protection services.

This chapter then is concerned with three groups of families:

- those who are in receipt of support services because the health or development of a child is likely to be significantly impaired or further impaired without the provision of services (Section 17, 10b), but who are not actually suffering or shown to be likely to suffer significant harm at the time when services are requested;

- those where there is reason to believe that the child may be suffering significant harm or is likely to do so, and an enquiry leading to a child protection conference is underway;

- those where a protection conference has concluded that the child is suffering or likely to suffer significant harm, and a multi-agency plan and registration are necessary.

The nature of partnership in these three sets of circumstances will in many respects be similar but in some important respects will be different.

Much of what follows is based on our research on family involvement in child protection work in seven authorities and draws heavily on the views of parents, children, social workers and managers interviewed for that project (Thoburn et al, 1992 and forthcoming).

Working in Partnership in Child Protection: The Research Evidence
Since the child protection conference is so central to child protection work, it is inevitable that practice around the time of the conference and at the conference itself sets the tone for the rest of the work. There are now a large number of small-scale studies, most unpublished, which conclude that family members do not feel involved in the work if they are excluded from the conferences. (See Lewis, 1992 for details of some of these.) The studies also show that the majority of professionals consider that conferences, (and indeed the child protection work as a whole), are more effective when family members are invited to attend. Parents themselves are also clear that partial involvement, whilst better than nothing, still leaves them feeling that attempts to involve them are merely tokenistic at best, and at worst reinforce the sense of exclusion and powerlessness. In a small number of cases partial family involvement is counter-productive in that it brings home to parents the existence of a group of powerful people who are talking about them, and making plans for their lives, without them being able to exert influence, or correct misapprehensions.

The study on which this chapter is based took this earlier research forward by focusing on all aspects of the first six months of the work. We were also concerned with the involvement of all family members: the alleged abuser if he or she was involved in a parenting role at the time of the allegation; the non-abusing parent or carer, if the two can be separated; a parent who is in contact but living elsewhere, and the child.

Working Together makes clear that the Children Act guidance to work *in partnership* with family members in order to help children in need applies in cases where the child is in need of protection, as well as for other children in need. Paragraph 6.5 states that:

> the initial child protection conference brings together *family members and professionals* from the agencies which are concerned with child care and child protection *to share and evaluate* the information gathered during the investigation, to *make decisions* about the level of risk to the children, to *decide on the need for registration* and to *make plans* for the future (our emphasis).

Paragraph 6.11 emphasises that:

> The involvement of children and adults in child protection conferences will not be effective unless they are fully involved from the outset in all stages of the child protection process, and unless from the time of referral there is as much openness and honesty as possible between families and professionals.

The question which we posed in the study reported here, therefore, was not 'Should social workers attempt to involve parents and older children in our child protection work?', but '*How* can they do it in such a way that it enhances practice and thus benefits the children and their families and in what sorts of cases is participatory practice more difficult or impossible to achieve because it detracts from the ability to safeguard and promote the welfare of a particular child?'

Design of the Research
A cohort of 220 consecutive cases was identified at the initial child protection conference in seven area teams, mainly in the south-east but including a midland county and a northern city. They were chosen because all expressed an interest in achieving greater involvement of parents and children, but they were choosing different ways of doing this. This applied especially to their policies on the invitation of family members to child protection conferences. In a fifth of the cases (44), at least one parent attended the whole of the initial or transfer conference, and in 36 cases (16 per cent) at least

one parent was present for most of the conference. In a quarter of cases the parent(s) were only invited at the end or to a small part, and the remaining 84 (38 per cent) did not attend, mostly because it was not departmental policy to invite them.

This aspect apart, the cases were very similar to those described in national statistics (DH 1992). The majority of the children were living at home throughout the six month period, and in 104 cases (almost a half) with the abuser or alleged abuser. In 61 cases (27 per cent) the index child (the oldest child in each family of those believed to have been abused) lived away from home for most of the time, either in care (19 per cent) or with relatives (8 per cent). The conference decided to register the child in 61 per cent of the cases, deferred a decision in six cases, and decided not to register in 36 per cent of the cases. In 19 of the cases there was a serious physical injury (including one death); four involved severe neglect, 16 involved penetrative sexual abuse; and 26 others were rated as severe or potentially life threatening. One hundred and fifty-two (including 23 cases of excessive punishment) did not come into the above categories (almost 70 per cent). This is not to deny the serious impact which abuse of any kind may have on a child, but to show that the majority of cases were not in the most serious categories.

The cases were studied mainly through an examination of social work records and questionnaires completed by social workers, parents, and in a small number of cases the children. In addition, a small sample of 33 randomly selected cases was studied in greater depth. These cases together with a further 38 where parents completed questionnaires and nine where children completed questionnaires provided us with a sample of 77 cases on which we had information from at least two sources, one of which was a parent or child, about the extent and nature of family involvement in the work, which could be set against the background of the full cohort. Although in the research we considered the involvement of children as well as parents, we concentrate in this chapter on working in partnership with *parents*. Our focus was on the role of social workers and social services departments although we also received the families members' comments on the work of other professionals.

The Meaning of Partnership
Our study began before the stronger mandate for family involvement appeared in *Working Together* and the agencies felt that they had more discretion about the extent and means of achieving parental involvement. It seemed important initially to consider the reasons given by those who were changing their practice and policies in order to work towards partnership with family members.

After extensive discussions with managers and practitioners, and consideration of the literature, three overlapping position statements were identified. A fourth has been added subsequently. The first, which we call 'the civil libertarian' or 'citizenship' position, holds that:

> Parents have a right as citizens to attend and give their views at meetings which can make important decisions about them and their children, and to hear what it is which the professionals are concerned about and what it is believed can be done to improve the situation.

As one social worker put it:

> 'The thing that's had most influence on my attitudes towards involving families has been a deep-held belief in treating parents or carers as I would wish to be treated myself.'

The 'professional' or 'effectiveness' argument can be summarised as:

> Most children on child protection registers live at home. Since the major partners in protecting children are therefore the parents or carers, it is more efficient and effective to involve them in important decision-making meetings.

A mother said:

> 'If I'd have been there I could have saved them a lot of time and a lot of money. I could have saved myself a lot of stress.'

The third general position statement we have described as the 'therapeutic view':

> Parents of children who are involved in child protection situations often have low self-esteem. Involving them in conferences and other aspects of work may diminish their sense of powerlessness and the tendency towards depression and 'learned helplessness'. If they feel more competent, their self-esteem will rise and they will be more able to work with professionals to improve the care of their children.

Another mother said:

> 'That's what I like. I feel part of it. I don't feel pushed out of the way. Normally, if I'm in a crowd I clam up if I don't know people.'

The fourth, which has become more apparent as agencies have been successful in working with parents, and is linked to the 'effectiveness' argument is:

> It is an incontrovertible fact that family members know more about their family life than any professional can know. They therefore have unique, special knowledge to contribute to the discussion about the best way to protect the child.

A social worker said about the mother's cohabitee:

> 'I remember putting it to him, that although he was a recent part of the family, he saw himself as a partner to Mrs. Thomas. He very much was involved and could say at firsthand what he thought would be helpful.'

This initial exploratory phase of the research led to a typology of family involvement based on Arnstein's 'ladder' (1969) illustrated in Table 1. Arnstein's work was essentially concerned with the consumer movement and community work, and therefore needs to be applied both to practice with individuals and families, and also to the particular circumstances of child protection work with its issues of authority and control.

Table 1
Degrees of Parental Involvement

Involvement in service design and monitoring	
Delegated power	
Partnership	
Participation	
Involvement	Those most usually found in child protection work
Consultation	
Keeping fully informed	
Manipulation	(non-participation/tokenism)
Placation	

Although not listed under the four different arguments just mentioned, as we are only concerned with genuine attempts at engaging the participation of family members, we have certainly found some arguments in favour of parental involvement which could come under the headings of 'placation' and 'manipulation'. Social workers have told us that they occasionally use a participatory style of work, not from a belief in partnership, but in order to create a trusting relationship with parents so that they can gain more information to collect evidence and move the case 'up-tariff' and towards court proceedings. Although expressing some discomfort, those doing so justify this approach with the argument that the first priority is to protect the child. At the other end of the scale, we have found few examples of agencies and area child protection committees involving families in the *design* of child protection services. Equally, it would be inappropriate to find a total delegation of power to either parents or children in individual child protection cases or in running the child protection service. Some agencies do work closely with Parents' Aid groups when children are in care, or with local groups of Parents Against Injustice (PAIN, 1991).

Our study was principally concerned with the middle 'rungs' of the ladder. Keeping family members fully informed is a basic minimum requirement if the practice is to be seen as at all participatory, whilst at the top end of the scale 'partnership' includes participation, consultation, involvement, and keeping fully informed.

In a training pack on partnership commissioned by the Department of Health, the Family Rights Group (1991) defines partnership as:

> marked by respect for one another, role divisions, rights to information, accountability, competence and value accorded to individual input. In short, each partner is seen as having something to contribute, power is shared, decisions are made jointly, and roles are not only respected but also backed by legal and moral rights. (FRG, 1991).

The Limits to Partnership

It will immediately be apparent that, using this strong definition of 'partnership', it will not be possible in all child protection cases to involve parents fully as partners. Indeed, in a small minority it may be harmful or even dangerous to the child even to keep an alleged abuser fully informed in the very early stages of an inquiry. As indicated in the introduction, the worker needs to be clear about the extent to which a parent is free to make choices about whether he or she will accept a service, and about the nature of the service, and should discuss this with the parent. This will depend on the type and stage of the case, and on the legal mandate, and is an essential part of the process of negotiating an agreement about how the investigation is to be conducted and about the protection plan. As one social worker put it:

> 'It takes you into the area of social work which is now so important— negotiation. Child protection is about negotiation.'

In recognition of the fact that partnership will be more difficult to achieve in some cases than in others, we allocated each to a 'worst scenario', a 'best scenario' or a 'middle' group. Thus if the parents welcome social work help, accept that there is a problem, agree with the social worker about the nature of abuse and the degree of harm, and about the way to proceed to improve the situation, it would be difficult for the worker *not* to engage in participatory practice. On the other hand a worker striving very hard to achieve parental involvement may not succeed if parents deny that abuse or neglect has taken place, if parents and social workers disagree about the degree of harm and ways of helping, if parents reject social work involvement (particularly if they have behaved violently towards social workers in the past). One of the questions we have posed in the research, to which we do not as yet have an answer, is whether some types of abuse make it harder to achieve involvement of parents than others. Fifty-nine (27 per cent of the sample) were initially rated by the researchers as 'best scenario' cases; 97 (44 per cent) were in the middle group, and 61 (28 per cent) were rated as coming into the 'worst scenario' category—with whom partnership might be hardest to achieve.

The Extent of Participatory Practice
In considering whether the practice which we were monitoring was participatory, we looked at both individual social work practice, and at the agency procedures. We concluded that it is essential for both to be participatory if the possibility is to be maximised of parents and agency working in partnership to protect the children.

Turning first to agency policies and procedures, in only three cases did we rate the agency's policy and procedures in the partnership category, using the strong FRG definition cited above, whilst in 37 per cent of cases they were rated as strongly participatory, and in 22 per cent moderately participatory. These ratings were based on the extent to which departmental policy and the actual management of the case encouraged and resourced the provision of clear information about child protection procedures, available support services, shared recording and access to records, and complaints procedures, as well as the extent to which they encouraged parental involvement at the investigation stage and attendance at child protection conferences. It should be noted that the agencies were specifically chosen because of their intention of working in partnership with families—thus the point must be made that even when agency policy has the expressed aim of working in partnership, the policy interpreted in individual cases may look very different.

In considering whether social work practice was participatory we were guided by what the workers told us and by evidence on file such as conference minutes, agreements and letters indicating that parents were consulted and their views taken into account. We also incorporated into our rating scheme what the familes told us about the sort of practice which helped them to become involved. Our study threw up little which will come as any surprise to anyone familiar with the literature about effective social work practice. We heard the usual pleas for social workers to be honest, to be clear about what is expected of the parents, and what the social worker is able to offer by way of help. Parents also want to feel that the social workers care about them as people as well as about their children. Compare this mother's comment:

> 'The social worker is only concerned about her own benefits and of doing her job correctly. Likewise, the health visitor. No-one really cares about the parents in these situations. I also felt as if they were laughing at me behind my back'.

with:

> 'When the social workers left, we parted as friends not as clients. We knew they were going to go. The new social worker has started to form a relationship with my daughter, and they go out together. That's fine by me.'

When translating these general principles of good practice to child protection work, perhaps the most important point to arise is the importance of the investigating social worker and the key worker combining practical help and emotional support with the other aspects of their protection work from the very start of the case. We found several examples of social workers who told parents that they would complete the investigation and the risk assessment before providing any form of help. To parents, this way of proceeding evidenced a lack of care about them and their children, which militated against their becoming successfully engaged in the work.

A father said:

> 'After the conference I thought, thank goodness for that. I'll do anything for my kids. It was weeks before I got a letter. I was left alone all that time until the assessment started weeks later.'

Thus parents and children described 'us and them' situations with the power firmly in the hands of the social workers, but the parents and children doing their best to guess the right answers to the assessment questions so as to get the social workers 'off their backs' as quickly as possible.

> 'I suppose *they* would call it support or help, but all they were doing was carrying on with their programme. It was *their* agenda of what *they* wanted to cover.'

> 'They didn't know what was going on under the surface. I wasn't going to tell them. And the children weren't going to tell them because they didn't want to lose their daddy. I didn't want to lose my husband.'

This was unfortunate since in several cases it was quite clear that parents and children could have benefited from a negotiated social work service, including practical help, emotional support, and help with difficult behaviour and relationships. In other words the psycho-social casework service which should be at the heart of social work help for families whose care of their children is slipping below acceptable standards was often withheld in the early stages of the case, making it more difficult to engage family members in the protection plan.

The researchers rated the social work practice as involving the parent who was the main carer in 47 per cent of cases (although this was considered to amount to participation or partnership in only 17 per cent of cases).

When agency policy and practice were combined, there were very few cases where both the practice of the worker and the policy and procedures of the agency could be placed in the partnership category. However, in 115 of the cases (52 per cent), the work of the social worker and the procedures of the agency were rated jointly as high or medium in terms of participatory practice; in a further 25 per cent of cases the social workers' practice was rated as high or medium, but the agency procedures were rated as low, whilst in 16 cases the agency procedures were rated highly, but the social workers' practice was rated as low in participation. Finally, in 13 per cent of cases both agency procedures and social workers' practice were rated as low in participation.

To say that the practice and procedures were participatory is not the same as saying that the parent was actually involved in the work. In only three cases could it be said that, using the FRG definition, the combined efforts of agency, worker and parent resulted in the work to protect the child being undertaken in partnership. In only 41 per cent of the cases did the researchers consider in the light of all the evidence available that the parent was definitely involved in the protection process and the work undertaken, whilst this could be said to be the case to some extent, or at the same time, in a further

50 per cent of cases. In some cases this was due to the determination of the parent, and despite the less than participatory practice of the agency or worker. In other cases, although practice *aimed at* involving the parents, their involvement was not achieved. We have evidence from 73 parents as to whether they themselves felt that they had been involved in the work. Seventeen (almost a quarter of these) said they were not involved at all, whilst 24 (33 per cent) said they *were* involved, and 32 (44 per cent) said they were involved to some extent or at some time. The social workers themselves considered they had successfully involved the main parent at all stages in 25 per cent of cases. In another 10 per cent of cases they thought the parent was involved in the early stages of the case but not later, whilst in 30 per cent of cases this pattern was reversed, with a move towards greater participation as the case progressed.

Factors Most Likely to Lead to Parental Involvement

We are still in the process of analysing the data to help us understand whether certain types of abuse or characteristics of parents, agency policies or social work practice appear to be associated with successfully involving the parents. However, it is already clear that our early hypotheses about the sorts of cases where it will be difficult to work in partnership with parents (the 'worst scenario' cases referred to earlier) are supported by our findings.

There are also some clear findings about agency policy and social work practice. The first point to be made is that agency policies and procedures which are participatory have to go hand-in-hand with social work practice which aims at working in partnership with parents. The first step is for the area child protection committee (ACPC) to agree on and resource a policy of family involvement in child protection work, including the routine invitation of parents to the whole of child protection conferences in all but a small number of cases. ACPCs and their member agencies then need to provide appropriate written material for parents and children who may attend, those who may support them at the meetings, and the various professional groups who will either attend or submit written reports. Each agency then needs to have a clear protocol about who should do what in preparation for the conference, and this is especially so for the social services department. In particular there must be clarity about the role of the investigating social worker, the team leader, and the chair of the conference. It is also important that there is a clear policy on the provision of minutes to those who attend the conference or are invited, and procedures to be followed if a parent wishes to make a complaint. Each agency should provide leaflets explaining procedures for recording, access to recorded information kept on file about them, and complaints, as well as the child protection procedures themselves. Agencies must also provide information about the availability of interpreters, and of any special equipment for those who have hearing loss, or special facilities for other parents who have disabilities. Parents will need information about the agency's policy for providing transport to meetings, and on child care facilities or expenses.

Effects of Parental Involvement on the Children

Before allocating a case to the successful outcome category, that is, one where the parent had been successfully involved in the work, it was important to consider whether there was any evidence to suggest that a child had been harmed as a result of the effort to work in partnership. Social workers were asked if they considered the outcome for the child was better, worse or no different as a result of parental involvement, or lack of involvement. Files were also scrutinised for any indication that participatory practice with the parents had had any impact on the outcome for the child. In such a short timescale, these assessments are likely to be little more than opinions. However, neither the social workers nor the file search revealed any indication that children had been harmed as a result of the involvement of their parents. In two cases the researchers rated the outcome for the child as worse as a result of parental involvement, and in 7 cases as possibly worse, whereas in 58 cases it was rated as better. This needs to be set against the researchers' assessment that in 20 cases the outcome for the child was worse as a result of *lack* of parental involvement.

There are clear indications that in most cases where parents were involved this had been of benefit, most obviously because it had led to more clarity in the work that was being undertaken. Sometimes this allowed for a more speedy resolution to the problems, whilst in other cases long-term plans for the child were able to be made more quickly, again because of the clarity which family involvement brought to the case.

Conclusion

Our study has indicated that working in partnership with parents in the early stages of child protection cases is not easy, even when the agency and individual workers are making serious attempts to do so. However, we can argue from our data that the effort is worth making since we saw evidence that, even in some difficult and complex cases, workers and parents were beginning six months after the case opened to work together in the interests of the child.

References

Arnstein, S. R., (1969) 'A ladder of participation' *Journal of the American Institute of Planners*, July, 1969.

Department of Health, (1991) *Working Together under the Children Act 1989.* London: HMSO.

Department of Health, (1991) *The Children Act 1989 Guidance and Regulations: Volume 2.* London: HMSO.

Department of Health, (1989) *Children and Young Persons on Child Protection Registers Year Ending 31 March 1989 England.* London: Government Statistical Service.

Family Rights Group, (1991) *The Children Act 1989: Working in partnership with families—A Training pack.* London: HMSO

Lewis, A. (1992) 'An overview of research into participation in child protection work' in J. Thoburn (ed.) *Participation in Practice: A Reader.* Norwich: University of East Anglia.

Parents Against Injustice, (1991) *Working in Partnership: Coping with an Investigation of Alleged Abuse or Neglect.* Stansted: PAIN.

Thoburn, J., Lewis, A. and Shemmings, D. (1992) *Family Involvement in Child Protection Conferences.* Norwich: University of East Anglia.

Thoburn, J., Lewis, A. and Shemmings, D. (in preparation) *Family participation in child protection: A report for the Department of Health.* Norwich: University of East Anglia.

CHAPTER 5

Family Support Services and Children with Disabilities

Pauline Hardiker

Introduction

This chapter outlines a framework for analysing family support services for children with disabilities. It explores the different functions of local authorities as providers and enablers, locates different types of services (counselling and respite care) in their social policy contexts, and identifies some ways forward.

The 1989 Children Act can be viewed and implemented in positive and promotional ways for children with disabilities. The preventive duty is broader and phrased more positively in terms of support for families rather than preventing, say, the need to provide accommodation. Nevertheless, the duty is owed to a restricted group of children, i.e. "children in need" (Masson, 1989). "Need" is defined very specifically in Section III. A child is defined as being in need if:

(a) he is unlikely to achieve or maintain, or to have the opportunity of achieving or maintaining, *a reasonable standard of health or development* without the provision for him of services by a local authority under this Part [of the Act].

(b) his *health or development* is likely to be *significantly impaired*, or further impaired, without the provision for him of such services; or

(c) he is *disabled*. ["A child is disabled" if he is blind, deaf or dumb, or suffers from a mental disorder of any kind, or is substantially and permanently handicapped by illness, injury or congenital deformity, or such other disability as may be prescribed"].

Many authorities, of course, use the contemporary terms 'children with special needs' or 'children with disabilities' with their less stigmatising connotations. Children with disabilities may also come under other provisions in the Act, such as those related to child protection and court proceedings, but these are not the main focus of this chapter.

The definition of children in need raises the question of why disability should be singled out in this way. The main reason is that the Children Act brings together the private and the Public law in relation to children, and this separate classification is a means by which the disability sections of old legislation (e.g. 1948 National Assistance Act) can be brought within its remit. Otherwise, children with disabilities could have been defined as "in need" under the generic standards of health and development. Furthermore, there is a dimension of positive discrimination here, because for the first time children with disabilities are given the same, plus additional, rights as all children to services, to be considered as children first and for their welfare to be a paramount consideration. Since other value stances of the Act (spelled out in the Guidance and Regulations) refer to normalisation, consultation, partnership, empowerment and anti-discrimination, the potential for positive action in the provision of family support services is truly great. When we ask what services do families and children with disabilities need and what strengths rather than what deficiencies do they have, this is further affirmation of the positive, promotional ethos and intention underlying support services for them.

The Children Act makes a clear distinction between ordinary services and compulsory interventions, and this is very important in respect of services for children with disabilities. The non-interventionist principle and the thresholds identified for state care and supervision relate to compulsory interventions, not to ordinary services. Therefore, compulsory orders for children with disabilities should be based on a philosophy of minimum necessary intervention; even when interventions are necessary, parental responsibility can be shared with the local authority and children and parents should be consulted about their needs and wishes. Support for families is conceived of in terms of ordinary services such as: domiciliary help, family centres, befriending schemes, day care provision and accommodation, and help in cash or kind. These support services should be mobilised wherever possible before compulsory interventions are considered.

Having established the priority to be given to ordinary services, support for families of children with disabilities can be provided for different purposes:

• to enable them to use universal provisions, such as health, education, housing, employment and leisure services, and to participate in community development and self-help initiatives.

• to enable them to use day care, family centres, respite care and befriending and counselling/casework services.

- to enable them to participate in supportive and therapeutic services should their children be at serious risk of abuse or invalidism, or their familial and social functioning be on the verge of breakdown.

- to enable them to share parental responsibility should their children need to be accommodated, in care, rehabilitated, hospitalised, or placed in permanent substitute care.

The overall value base underlying family support services in these different contexts is premised upon the need to pre-empt a more intrusive intervention or a disadvantageous outcome. It is, of course, not all straightforward either to define or to predict what is a more intrusive intervention. For example, when the risk of abuse is identified, this has to be balanced against the known risks of intervention, such as the trauma of removing a child and loss of confidence by the parents (Gardner, 1990). Doing nothing at an early stage of problem-development may lead to the need for "too much" intervention subsequently; doing "too much" may lead to abandonment by a family if the intervention is not followed up by careful, long-term planning with parents.

For example, the provision of accommodation may be too intrusive an intervention if a family of a child with a disability needs domiciliary services; on the other hand, the provision of accommodation on a well-planned basis may prevent a more negative outcome such as long-term separation between parents and child or drift in the system. If racist services are provided, this may lead a family to withdraw from a much-needed facility. If no service is provided, e.g. ordinary support, this may lead to the need for heavy interventions because, for example, significant harm has occurred. If families are not supported in the care of their child with a disability, this may lead to premature invalidism.

The spirit of the Children Act aims to generate flexible and positive thinking about the purposes of family support services, which should be carefully planned and provided in relation to different levels of need. A complementary value base enshrined in the Act (Schedule 2, paragraph 59) requires local authorities to provide services for children with disabilities, which are designed to minimise the effects of their disabilities and to give them the opportunity to lead lives that are as normal as possible.

It behoves all responsible agencies accordingly to address the values underlying the Children Act when planning, implementing monitoring and evaluating family support services for children with disabilities.

The Social Policy Contexts of
Family Support Services

Several aims and targets for family support services for disabled children have already been alluded to, but these now need to be located rather more firmly in their social policy contexts. They will be analysed in relation to bases for welfare and levels of intervention, using a framework developed by Hardiker, Exton and Barker [1991a, 1991b].

Bases for Welfare

The role and purpose of Personal Social Services can be considered in relation to the values which underpin the political, economic and legal institutions which legitimate them. Three bases for welfare will be examined: last resort, needs-based and multiple-interventions.

Minimum Necessary Intervention in Families [Last resort]

The care of children is not considered to be the proper business of the State, and parents are seen to be responsible for difficulties in childrearing. Parental rights and duties are stressed and the State only intervenes as a last resort or safety net when parenting or children's behaviour/development reaches damaging levels. This approach was recognisable in the Poor Law and it could re-emerge if family support services are not developed in line with the enabling philosophy of the Children Act. If children with disabilities are first subject to interventions because significant harm has been established and the source is located in deficient parenting, this basis for welfare is evident.

Family Support Services [Recognition of needs]

The normality of difficulties in rearing children in a complex and changing society is acknowledged here, and the State is given a greater role in providing services to supplement and support families. Children's services aim to reintegrate children and families into society rather than to rescue children and punish parents. Family support services are, therefore, given a high profile in the contexts of undertaking professional assessments of needs, working directly with children in partnership with parents, and providing flexible packages of care.

The importance of maintaining and supporting children with disabilities within their own families (however broadly these are defined, especially in respect of different social and ethnic groups) is stressed alongside enabling families to use supportive services.

Multiple Interventions [Addressing social disadvantages]
In this approach, social problems (including many parenting and child care difficulties) are seen to be the product of social inequalities. The Personal Social Services play a role in addressing social disadvantages. Social work, accordingly, is a multi-role activity which includes casework advocacy, mediation, empowerment and community participation. [Sometimes social inequalities are addressed more thoroughly in terms of class, gender, ethnicity and disabilities; anti-oppressive practices are then seen as a hallmark of social work; Macdonald, 1991]. The chapter by Westcott in this book and the Honeylands example illustrate this basis for welfare.

The Children Act can be interpreted in this way, especially in relation to family support services and disabilities. For example, the following principles of good practice are outlined in the Guidance and Regulations: giving parents more power vis a vis the local authority and enhancing their strengths; listening to children and addressing their rights; taking account of the wishes and views of the local community including user groups, and anti-discrimination. For example some Social Services Departments are developing schemes for involving disabled children and their families in self assessments of their needs (See Agency D, below).

These three bases of welfare outline some of the different social policy territories inhabited by family support services for children with disabilities. State intervention is never as simple and clear-cut, however, as these distinct approaches imply because there are overlaps. The concept of parental responsibility can be interpreted in terms of minimum necessary intervention, or support for families in relation to needs, or multiple interventions to address social dis-advantages. Hopefully, the latter interpretations will prevail, especially when parental responsibility is shared with the local authority. Furthermore, state interventions are multi-dimensional and interlocking, including central and local government and the crucial role of the voluntary, informal and private sectors.

Levels of Intervention
Levels of intervention are a further means of locating different types of family support services for children with disabilities. The four levels outlined identify stages in the development of problems and targets for intervention.

First Level [Universal]
This level of intervention is intended to stop problems arising in the first place, through providing universal services (income, housing,

education, employment, health) to populations. More specifically for Social Services Departments, the problems are associated with those of entering a client career and becoming dependent on the agency and compulsory interventions and, thus, possibly, stigmatised. This is an enormous topic, but suffice it to say that this level of service is geared to *vulnerable* populations, communities and families, and to diverting families of children with disabilities to universal and community provisions wherever possible. Targets for intervention include inter-professional collaboration in relation to local authority-wide services, and to other services such as health and voluntary agencies (e.g. Honeylands). Advice, guidance and signposting services in health centres and schools are also relevant. Direct interventions include community development, networking and self-help, with the aim of empowering families and strengthening their own support networks.

Second Level [Early intervention]
These interventions address early risk groups, such as families in temporary crisis or those in early difficulties; the risk of family breakdown or child deterioration is relatively low. The targets of intervention are mainly families, the approaches based on short-term, task-centred or crisis intervention methods. The aim is to restore personal and social functioning, so that direct interventions by Social Services Departments are no longer required and the families can be returned to first level service provision.

Families of children with disabilities are likely to experience normal life crises such as bereavement, illness, external stresses, behavioural and relationship difficulties; these may or may not be connected with their child's disabilities but they may affect parenting capacities temporarily. Children with disabilities may also be vulnerable to abuse (see Westcott). Generic social work methods, including casework, behavioural and group work may be appropriate in these circumstances alongside the provision of flexible packages of care. For example, the chapter by Quine in this book illustrates a behavioural programme for families of children with severe learning difficulties and disturbed patterns of sleep.

Third Level [Remedial interventions]
Interventions at this level are targeted on heavy-end risk groups where there is a prospect of family breakdown. Families may have severe and well-established difficulties/needs and there may be high risk of significant harm. A range of approaches and resources may be used to address the worst effects of chronic difficulties or to prevent more serious problems, such as long-term separation of

children from their parents. Where there are children with disabilities in a family, such serious thresholds may arise for a variety of reasons: a family which has exhausted its coping resources and supportive networks, terminal illness, multiple and serious life-events which may or may not be associated with the children's disability.

Helping interventions aim to restore personal and family functioning, to provide a range of respite and community care facilities or to plan for periods in care or hospital. Work at this level presents great challenges to all concerned, but the overall aim is to keep the disabled child's place and/or identity with her family, to reduce stresses and/or possible harm to the child.

Fourth Level [Rehabilitation or damage limitation]

This level relates primarily to children who have entered the care system or those for whom severe past problems have been identified. Interventions aim to reduce the degree of harm or disadvantage which may arise from being accommodated or in care, and to rehabilitate children either to their natural families or to substitute care; for children with disabilities this may involve planning for hospital care and/or different forms of residential care. The aim for children with disabilities who have been abused may be to provide counselling in order to reduce any harmful effects and to help them to recover [see Westcott's chapter]. The work requires skilled interventions: psychosocial assessments, direct work with children, maintaining links, partnerships with parents, and social care planning. Liaison with a range of health care, voluntary and educational services may also be necessary. Much of the work is indirect, including interprofessional collaboration. The local authority functions here as enabler and provider.

This exposition of bases for welfare and levels of intervention has located different aims and sites for social work and family support, in relation to children with disabilities. These issues will now be brought into sharper focus by outlining some profiles of intervention.

Profiles of Intervention

If bases for welfare and levels of intervention are combined, it is easy to argue that the welfare base of the service indicates the *preferred* level of intervention to be targeted:

- multiple interventions target
  first level (universal) needs;

• family support services target
  second level/early risk groups;

• minimum necessary interventions target
  third level/heavy-end risk groups.

However, the message of the Children Act is that local authorities as
providers and enablers should develop services in relation to every
level of need and risk; more priority should be given than hitherto
to ordinary services, at first and second levels of intervention. This
is important, especially if one considers the distortions which
occurred in some Social Services Departments owing to the priority
given to child abuse and child protection; some families only
received a service if child abuse was identified, and sometimes the
interventions were too intrusive.

    There can be no guarantee, of course, *in respect of individual
families*, that the provision of first and second level services prevents
the need for third level ones. Nevertheless, it is important to build
such preventive aims for vulnerable populations and risk groups
into the strategic objectives of Social Services Departments.

    Furthermore, each child with a disability and their family
receives different levels of service with diverse elements of provision
combined in a variety of ways. Most children with disabilities will
require a service for life from a multiplicity of professionals and
agencies which will meet their ongoing needs and those arising from
temporary or crisis situations. Therefore, in order to maintain a
flexible pattern of response, a combination of supportive services
and interventions is required: those provided directly by a Social
Services Department team; packages of care arranged with other
agencies, and enabling approaches to encourage use of community-
wide resources. This method of providing a range of direct and
indirect interventions across local authority and community-wide
services enables a Social Services Department to give priority to, say,
children   with   substantial   and   permanent   disabilities;
simultaneously, the Social Services Department can be *available*
when necessary to all families of children with disabilities in an
endeavour to prevent or delay high dependence on scarce resources.

> "Parents are normally very pleased to work in partnership at all stages.
> There is very little tendency to become overdependent on the agency
> unless this is necessary for the welfare of the child and the continued
> viability of the family". [SSD Position Statement].

Selected examples are now presented of some ways in which Social
Services Departments and Voluntary Agencies are developing

family support services for children with disabilities, targeting on every level of intervention in the true spirit of the Children Act.

Agency A: Northamptonshire

This Social Services Department is developing a care management approach towards its services for children with disabilities. The agency is attempting to ensure that Children's Services and Adult Services adopt a common approach to meeting the needs of service users; it is also aiming to bring work with children with disabilities into the mainstream of the agency's services for children in addition to developing a specialist function to prioritise this group of children.

Policies, procedures and practices identify the need for a continuum of care services in relation to children with disabilities. This should include: family support services → respite care through 'family link' and specialist respite care units → medium/ long-stay provision in county → specialist agency placements out-county. The intention is to shift the distribution of resources to the development of good quality *local* support services to enable families to care for their children with appropriate help. Service developments are planned in relation to two jointly-funded Education/Social Services Department projects. Firstly, a six place respite care unit with a focus on autism. Secondly, a small residential unit for children unable to live with their families and awaiting foster placement. Some residential respite care facilities are to cease in their current form and resources are to be redistributed to fund planned developments.

The backbone of these provisions are family support services where the Care Managers are located. Six new Care Manager posts have been created throughout the county; four are placed in Child Care Teams and work with school-age children, and two are based in hospital social work teams and work with children under five years. The Care Managers are directly involved in assessing individual families' needs and in commissioning and co-ordinating assessments from other professionals and in encouraging families to assess their own needs. Each Care Manager has a devolved budget with which to make spot purchases at a local level of the individualised element of service relevant for a particular family. Care Managers are also expected to develop a picture of aggregate need within the locality and to carry some responsibility for service developments. There are plans to appoint development workers to promote wider service responses.

Agency B: Leicestershire

This Social Services Department is responding positively to the implications of the Children Act in relation to the development of services for children with disabilities.

Background
The Area Health Authority, Education Department, Voluntary Agencies, the Social Services Department and representatives of users collaborated with the National Development Team to develop provision for children with severe learning difficulties. They have been planning for a comprehensive service and to integrate it with those for all children in need. Consideration has been given to the transition between children's and adult services and to the Statementing requirements of the Disabled Persons Act, 1986. The implications of the Children Act are outlined including: the need to take account of a child's racial, religious, cultural and linguistic background; partnerships with parents; duty to promote the upbringing of the child within their own family; the paramountcy of the child's welfare. Specific new duties are identified: minimising the effect of disability on children in their area; normalisation; opening and maintaining a register; planning of placements.

Shortcomings in the Social Services Department's current provision for children with disabilities are identified:

• lack of co-ordination and planning in provision of services for individual children;

• absence of clear access points or processes to receive services;

• inflexible provision which is service rather than needs led;

• provision of respite care in response to crises rather than supporting and assisting families;

• lack of focused or strategic interventions with families, apart from those designed to reduce the need for children to live away from home;

• insufficient range of respite care, especially with regard to choice and locality.

Service Principles
Fourteen principles are enumerated including: the rights of children with disabilities; the need to protect children with disabilities from abuse and exploitation; individualism; cultural and racially appropriate services; support for families; choice and normalisation; co-ordinated, flexible and locally accessible services; consultation, partnership, information, advocacy and representation; recognition and support for needs of carers; choice of least intrusive method of intervention into the lives of the children with their families.

These principles are identified more specifically in relation to strategic objectives:

- access to services.

- information strategy, including signposting services and information packs.

- contact point for information, assessments and services, through creation of six specific social worker posts designed to enhance the services.

- planning mechanisms to be co-ordinated through the specialist social workers and the new child care planning system; for example, new admissions to respite accommodation will be made through the Panel meetings and regular reviews undertaken subsequently.

1. Service Provision
A child with a disability is entitled to a *full assessment of* their individualised needs and provision of appropriate services. The definition of disability in the Act is considered to be archaic and offensive to many service users and is replaced by a more positive and enabling one:

- the child has a substantial and permanent physical, visual, hearing or intellectual impairment

- that resulting from this impairment, the child is limited or prevented from undertaking the daily living activities of their choice

- social and environmental factors affecting a child's level of disability are recognised, including physical access, resources and stigma.

The specialist social workers will co-ordinate thorough, comprehensive and inter-agency assessments.

2. Home Support Services

Children with disabilities may be referred for a home-care assistant; provision of a countywide sitting service for parents is being explored; creative use will be made of other family-based support services, e.g. family-aides, sponsored childminding or nursery and Family Centre places; referrals to specialist services (occupational and speech therapists); development of a range of out-of-school hours activities in partnership with voluntary organisations and user groups.

3. Provision of Respite Accommodation

The principles outlined above are repeated:

- Respite provision should be local, accessible and flexible. There should be a balance between family-based and residential provision, and the latter should be in small, normal housing units.

- Family-based respite care is to be developed by a family placement worker in each division; they will have a devolved budget and develop existing family-link schemes. This provision will cater for children with physical disabilities, severe learning difficulties and multiple disabilities. The need to recruit carers from minority ethnic communities is recognised.

- A number of small residential respite centres across the county will be developed to replace a large central provision. The Health Authority is expanding its respite provision for those children in need of nursing care. There are also proposals to develop a specialist, multi-disciplinary team and unit to address the needs of children with severe levels of challenging behaviour.

Timescales and Financial Implications

These are reviewed, including virement of resources from large to smaller residential provisions and implications of changed service arrangements with the Children's Society (see below). Use is made of Children Act growth monies and the provision of additional resources. Equal opportunities implications are addressed in relation to service users and providers.

Specific Plans in Respect of Locally-Based Respite Provision

The implications of these plans are outlined in detail. Work is being undertaken to collate the views of service users, parents and carers by an inter-agency working group. The mixed views of parents are acknowledged and note is made of the many parents of children with severe learning difficulties who do not use respite services because they are neither local nor accessible. Some of these children have not been consulted directly because of the nature of their disabilities.

Summary

These proposals address every level of intervention and the continuum of care in relation to children with disabilities. The importance of ordinary services is affirmed and priority is given to this user group through specialist provisions. The importance of authority-wide and other services is recognised. The value-base of the service is clearly spelled out and strategic objectives are identified. *Hopefully, procedures for implementing the new provisions will be developed alongside monitoring systems to evaluate outcomes.* The ways in which the Children Act can be used in a promotional way, positively to discriminate in the interests of children with disabilities, are clearly evident.

The 'S' Family

Services provided to this family illustrate some ways in which the strategies outlined above have been used positively to discriminate in their interests.

Ms S is a single parent who receives Income Support and Disability Living Allowance; she suffers from a chronic disease. Her first child was taken into care and is now grown up. Ms S's daughter, Debbie, is five and a half years old and is disabled through epilepsy and cerebral palsy; Debbie attended a community-based Family Centre and now attends a school for children with special needs, and has been statemented. Debbie walks with a splint on her leg, has delayed speech and wears nappies at night-time; she some-times displays difficult behaviour, which indicates some developmental delay. Debbie is doing very well in school.

There is a strong bond with her mother, who is very committed to Debbie (especially in the light of the history of her first child). Ms S and Debbie have a limited informal support network.

The social worker outlined the advantages of bringing children with disabilities into the frame of the Children Act, especially in relation to Debbie [Second level—early risk]:

1. It has made planning of regular support and respite care easier.

2. The aim is consistent with the philosophy of the Act, to keep mother and child together in the community.

3. Working in partnership with Debbie's mother has enhanced her strengths.

4. Through the provision of accommodation, Ms S has been empowered to plan for Debbie's respite care and to have her at home when she wants this. The previous provision of respite care on an emergency basis has been avoided.

5. The Panel System [reviewing requests for accommodation] and the Respite Planning Meeting have avoided unplanned care episodes and drift in care; they also provide predictable services, with a known time-scale. The Panel system also encourages the social worker to plan ordinary services in the community for Ms S and Debbie, e.g. support groups especially during school holidays and contacts with other families. There is informal contact with the foster carers between the provision of respite accommodation. The foster carers are accessible but do not live locally.

6. Debbie is coming on very well, and through the periods she spends in accommodation she is stimulated by the foster carers' own children.

7. The social worker thought that the Social Services Department's previous Child Care Strategy laid good foundations for the Children Act, so the service perhaps did not have as far to move as some others.

Voluntary Agency: Children's Society

Voluntary agencies offer services to children with disabilities and their families across the continuum of care, targeted on every level of intervention. For example, one project in Agency C offers a range of services, including the development of integrated pre-school provision and support for integrated holiday and playschemes in a predominantly rural area (first level); the project also has a small residential component for different forms of respite care (second and third levels). Another project provides residential care for children and young people with disabilities in ordinary houses next to each other in a city suburb (fourth level). One house provides for young people in care on a long-term basis; it will close shortly and the residents will be placed with families in the community. The other house provides short-term residential and day-care for children throughout the county; this house will also close shortly and be replaced by bungalows in local communities. The Agency is collaborating with Leicestershire Social Services Department (see above) to move away from the predominantly residential focus and towards family support services in the community for children and young people with disabilities.

Agency D—Dudley Metropolitan Borough

Context
The Bridge Team (Learning Disabilities) is one of five Community Teams jointly-financed by Health and Social Services. It is led by a Care Manager and includes community health nurses (priority health) and social workers (adult services). *It is developing services for children with disabilities* since the focus of the Social Services Department's children's teams is still mainly child protection. The team has established links with some voluntary agencies to provide residential services and also family support. There is no team budget but there are plans to develop a shadow budget to work out costings for purchasing services when a budget is eventually devolved. There is a Special Needs Register which is a very useful, comprehensive and well-resourced computer-based record of all people with learning disabilities (adults and children) known to the service. The system described below was first developed in relation to adults and the results of a monitoring-evaluation exercise have been very favourable. *The system is currently also being developed in relation to children with learning disabilities.*

The Individual Programme Planning System
The different component of this system are outlined below:
1. Flow Chart of the IPP Process:

Stage I *Individual* requiring IPP.

Stage II IPP *Co-ordinator* appointed.

Stage III *Co-ordinator works with* individual, their key worker and significant others to assess individual and their situation.

Stage IV *Strengths/Needs List* drawn up and *Quality Matrix* circulated to those invited to IPP meeting.

Stage V *IPP Meeting* held to agree Strengths/Needs assessment and agree individual future short and long term plans. Individuals responsible for goals are identified and time scales are set. Service deficiencies are identified and noted to central point (Special Needs Register). Date set for next IPP meeting.

Stage VI   *Co-ordinator monitors* goal achievements.

Stage VII   *Review.*

2.   Ten Point Standards of IPP (used mainly for staff training).

An IPP is a written plan which describes the future aims for work with a person which are relevant to that person's needs.

Start with **person's consent and involvement** (or if impossible, consent of nearest relative, carer, advocate).

Undertake an **Individual Needs Assessment.** This identifies the person's wants and wishes for their immediate and long-term future.

The Needs Assessment addresses all aspects of a person's life (home, work, education, leisure).

All the key people in a person's life are identified, and may be contacted and involved if the person so wishes.

Before an IPP is agreed, **a summary of the assessment** is presented in the form of a Strength/Needs List and possibly a Quality Matrix.

The IPP is finalised during a meeting. The format and procedure of the meeting is adapted as much as possible to the needs and wishes of the person whose IPP it is.

The Standard Form is completed at the end of the meeting which specifies:

• what aims were agreed
• who agreed to take responsibility for each aim
• time scale for achievement of each aim
• service deficiencies
• the person responsible for convening the next meeting

The Standard Form is sent to the **Special Needs Register.**

A Summary of the agreed aims is sent to those present at the meeting and any other key people identified by the client and the co-ordinator.

Future IPP Meetings must start off with a review of the progress made in achieving the aims set at the last meeting.

If the planning process is to be called an IPP, these ten standards must be met. However, it is hoped that the process will be as flexible and individualised as possible.

3. Comparison of IPP Process and Typical Service Review

    e.g. user-led rather than service led;
          individualised not standardised assessment;
          holistic not partial;
          users' key networks involved.

    The overall difference between the two systems may be characterised as service reviews being driven by the needs of the service managers to show that services are being conrolled, whilst IPPs should be based on the perspective of the individual user and put their needs first.

4. Workbook: Preparing for an IPP

    This Workbook is presented in straightforward words and pictorial language. The aim is to help the person to make plans for their future life.

    They are invited to list:

    *   the people they like
    *   the activities they like
    *   an active diary
    *   their preferred activities
    *   any issue they would like to talk about, including worries and lack of understanding of something.

    The IPP Meeting is then discussed.

5. Strengths/Needs List

    *   **Strengths:** e.g. health, verbal understanding, communication skills, activities and relationships (specified).

    *   **Needs:** e.g. further assessment and help to communicate person's needs; help and protection from common dangers; help with all aspects of dressing, washing; guidance with eating and drinking.

6. Quality Matrix

    This is completed in relation to home, work and leisure in respect of the following values: community presence, real mixing and participation, real choices, status and respect, competence. The Matrix is completed in terms of the extent to which the person's life currently matches the Quality Accomplishments.

7. Summary of IPP Meeting

    Clear aims are set, time scale, responsibilities, etc.

8. The IPP Manual

    This package provides background and instructions to staff about; for example:

    • the value-base, e.g. community presence, real choices

    • the people involved in the IPP process, including service user and advocate

    • role of the IPP Co-ordinator.

    • assessment and assessment tools; summary of the Strengths/Needs List and Quality Matrix.

    • preparing and chairing the meeting.

    • setting and writing clear aims.

The Social Policy Contexts
The Individual Programme Planning System is based on a philosophy which aims to empower users and carers and to advocate on their behalf especially in respect of shortfalls in services. The Strengths/Needs mode of assessment and Quality Matrix aim to identify positive aspects of a person's life and to address social inequalities. Deficits are turned into needs which require services and a multi-method, multi-level response. The IPP system is clearly targeted on First Level Intervention, i.e. for people with disabilities as a population or prioritised group. Individuals with disabilities and their families may receive services at every level of intervention. The Special Needs Register is also used as a positive device to monitor an individual user's pathways through the system and to develop a picture of aggregate need and response.

Summary

Even from the selected illustrations in this section, the diversity of organisational patterns developing in relation to children with disabilities is apparent. The Care Management System in Northamptonshire spans children and adult services, but services for children with disabilities are firmly located within the children's section with an additional specialism in order to prioritise this group of service users. In Leicestershire, children with disabilities clearly take their place within service developments under the Children Act, which are continuing the innovations started under an earlier Child Care Strategy; specialist workers and resources are created in order to make up for previous shortfalls in provision and to give priority to children with disabilities.

Services for children with disabilities are currently being developed in Dudley within a framework of adult services jointly funded by Social Services and Health Services. These differences in team boundaries and specialisms are very interesting in themselves; in Social Services Departments, services for children with disabilities will always have to span adult services because of the need to plan for the transition of service users from one to the other during their life-time. Many voluntary agencies (such as the Children's Society) are also redirecting provisions for children and young people with disabilities from a residential to a community-based focus. All these developments are consistent with the Children Act's stress on ordinary services, across a continuum of care, addressed at every level of intervention, and on inter-agency collaboration.

Ways Forward

It is not at all helpful if "family support" is used as a kind of spray on phrase, particularly if the aim is to criticise local authorities for not doing enough of it. As we have seen, diverse aims and types of family support services can be identified in relation to the different contexts of practice. Support to enable families to use universal services is rather different from support addressed at family breakdown or permanency planning, though they should all be based upon good practice principles. There is encouraging evidence of a variety of projects targeting on different levels of intervention, employing a range of direct methods alongside inter-agency and interprofessional collaboration. Workers in the disability field already have a wealth of experience and expertise in working with parents and children, assisting groups, collaborating with voluntary organisations and liaising with local authority-wide and other statutory services. Therefore, the first way forward for service providers is to build upon existing good practices and to identify the services' strengths and weaknesses.

Secondly, the classical social work maxim—partialise the problem—may be another useful step forward. The framework outlined, which locates family support in relation to bases of welfare and levels of intervention, is one useful device for partialising the issues. It may enable managers to locate which levels of intervention can be targeted through direct Social Services Department provision, and which through more indirect interventions, adopting an enabling role in relation to local authority wide services and other agencies. Furthermore, the identification of levels of intervention may be used as a tool for monitoring and evaluating services. For example, if "too many" children with disabilities are 'slipping through nets' and entering third level services because there is serious risk of significant harm, this should be cause for concern; strategies may then be developed to return many of these children to second and first level ordinary services, especially community-based ones, and to include early interventions in strategic service objectives aimed at preventing future risk of significant harm or family breakdown.

Thirdly, Social Services Departments have built up a great deal of expertise in developing and managing services, especially in relation to newly identified priority groups and approaches. These same systems could be developed (as they are being in the agencies described) in relation to the promotional objectives identified for family support services and children with disabilities in the Children Act. A Department of Health Survey (Robbins, 1990) found that reference to children with disabilities was generally absent from local authority policy statements (Macdonald, 1991). This should no longer be possible following the requirements, guidance and regulations of the Children Act. One way forward could be to use frameworks identified elsewhere [In Need Implementation Group, 1991]:

"Outline Strategy for Family Support Services for Children with Disabilities"

Values and Philosophy

1   Universalism.

2. Equality and Equity of Access to Services.

3. The Normality of Difficulties in Parenting.

4. Participation.

5. Normalisation.

6. Anti-discrimination.

Strategic Objectives
1. Services should be provided across the local authority and not confined to Social Services Departments.

2. Programmes should be established for assessing needs and monitoring unmet needs.

3. Family support services should provide packages of care along a continuum, addressing different levels of intervention, and using the mixed economy of welfare.

4. Mechanisms should be developed for representing the needs and wishes of children, their parents and wider networks.

5. There should be a Prospectus of Services and systems developed for representation, complaints and inspection.

6. Priority should be given to training in respect of anti-oppressive practices and support services for children with disabilities and their families.

Implementation
Procedures to secure the implementation of the strategic objectives should be established. These could relate to implementation of services targeted on different levels of intervention, or to the reasonable expectation which can be made of local authorities, managers, practitioners and families. Checklists of parents' and children's or carers' and users' rights may also be used as implementation procedures.

Evaluation
It is easy to understand why local authorities are currently targeting services at third and fourth levels of intervention. However, a change of thinking is required whereby first and second level interventions are seen as cost-effective in the long run; this will only be so if the message about the importance of ordinary, local authority-wide services and the mixed economy of welfare is fully

addressed. Social Services Departments are moving in the direction of being enablers as well as providers, and this is very relevant in relation to support services for children with disabilities and their families. They will still have a lead role in many areas, so social work and service delivery skills developed during the welfare state era will be needed as never before: psychosocial assessments, direct work with children, mobilising packages of care, family casework, advocacy and empowerment, community development and inter-professional collaboration. New skills will also need to be developed in user-defined needs-led assessments, care management and anti-discrimination policies and practices.

Appendix I suggests one format for evaluating the impact of family support policies on social work practices for children with disabilities.

Postscript

This chapter has argued that the different purposes and types of family support services for children with disabilities can be identified in relation to their underlying value base and the level of intervention targeted. For example, respite care can be offered proactively to prevent stress or as a crisis response to a family on the threshold of breakdown; packages of care can be provided flexibly in response to expressed needs or routinely in response to agency timetables. Furthermore, Social Services Departments may be the main providers of interventions such as specialist family therapy, group work or respite care, but also play a more enabling role in relation to local authority-wide services and the mixed economy of welfare. If the strategic objectives of these different services are clearly identified, they may be less precarious, less marginalised and less easy targets for cuts. Social Services Departments may no longer be able to provide outreach community development services *directly*, but they must still play important enabling roles at first and second levels of intervention. We may perhaps begin to learn more from one another as we face the challenges of the Children Act in relation to children with disabilities and their families.

APPENDIX

Evaluating Policy/Practice Links

This chapter has argued that *policies* to support families who have disabled children are not simple and homogeneous. It is necessary to identify the value base of the service and the levels targeted by direct and indirect Social Services Department interventions respectively. Their impact upon practices needs to be underpinned by outlining strategic objectives and implementation procedures. Hardiker, Exton and Barker (1991c) outlined one method of evaluating the links between policies and practices in preventive child care and this method could be developed in relation to family-support services for children with disabilities:

1. Identify the **broad frameworks** addressed: e.g. development of ordinary needs-based support services for families of children with disabilities targeted on early risk groups and on families where there is a serious risk of harm.

2. Specify dimensions of **political control and direction:** e.g. the role of the Social Services Department in relation to direct interventions, local authority wide services and the mixed economy of welfare, respectively; draw up a timetable for the achievement of strategic objectives.

3. Identify **methods of organisational control:** e.g. systems for planning, implementation, monitoring and evaluation.

4. Draw up systems for **representation, consultation and complaints:** e.g. forums for negotiation between members, officers and trades unions; avenues for consultation with children, parents, community members, user groups, and voluntary and private organisations; equal opportunities issues.

5. Outline systems for **virement in relation to services and resources:** e.g. identify mechanism by which resources saved through closing residential units will be secured to support community-based services.

6. Identify **areas of non-decision-making:** e.g. groups of children with disabilities not identified in the policies or not given adequate priority.

7. Specify possible **obstacles to service development:** e.g. resources and priorities; political and community mandates; different time scales of central and local governments; calculation of Standard Spending Assessments; need to develop more useful and relevant systems for evaluating effectiveness, especially in relation to different levels of intervention and to anti-discrimination.

References

Department of Health (1991a). *The Children Act 1989: Guidance and Regulations. Volume 2: Family Support, Day Care and Educational Provision for Young Children.* London, HMSO.

Department of Health (1991b). *The Children Act 1989: Guidance and Regulations. Volume 6: Children with Disabilities.* London, HMSO.

Gardner, R. (1990). "Prevention of family breakdown—a development project at National Children's Bureau". *Adoption and Fostering,* 14(4), 23-26.

Hardiker, P., Exton, K. & Barker, M. (1991a). *Policies and Practices in Preventive Child Care.* Alderhot, Gower.

Hardiker, P., Exton, K., & Barker, M. (1991b). "The social policy contents of prevention in child care". *British Journal of Social Work,* 21(4), 341-359.

Hardiker, P., Exton, K., & Barker, M. (1991c). "Analysing policy/practice links in preventive child care". In P. Carter, T. Jeffs & M. Smith (eds), *Social Work and Social Welfare Yearbook 3.* Milton Keynes, Open University Press.

In Need Implementation Group (1991). *The Children Act and Children's Needs: Make It The Answer—Not The Problem.* London, NCVCCO.

Macdonald, S. (1991). *All Equal under the Act.* London, Race Equality Unit, NISW.

Masson, J. (1990). *The Children Act 1989: Text and Commentary.* London, Sweet & Maxwell.

Robbins, (1990). *Child Care Policy: Putting It In Writing: A Review of English Authorities' Child Care Policy Statements.* London, SSI, HMSO.

Acknowledgements

I should like to thank the following people for helping me in the preparation of this chapter: Mary Barker, Jane Gibbons and Marjorie Thompson; officers in many local authority departments and voluntary agencies, especially those in agencies A, B, C and D for providing me with details about policy/practice developments; Lucy Panasiuk for her skill, patience and generosity in processing numerous drafts of the chapter.

CHAPTER 6

Vulnerability and the Need for Protection

Helen Westcott

Introduction

This chapter will discuss the role of family support in the protection of disabled children from abuse. That disabled children are in need of protection may seem surprising to some (Middleton, 1992), and the chapter begins with a brief description of studies indicating that, indeed, such is the case. Factors which influence the vulnerability of disabled children are discussed, with suggestions as to how risks in both familial and extra-familial settings may be reduced. Finally, a working example of one way in which co-ordinated family support services can be provided to families with disabled children is given before the implications of the Children Act for disabled children and their families are briefly drawn out.

For the purposes of this chapter the terms 'disabled' and 'with disabilities' will be used interchangeably to denote a child who has either a physical disability, or learning difficulty, or both. The terms thus encompass children with a wide variety of different needs, and it is important not to lose sight of the fact that each child is an individual irrespective of any needs he or she may have. As will be argued later, it is all too frequently the society within which children live that is disabling, more than any personal characteristic of the child.

The term 'vulnerability' refers here to a heightened suscepti-bility to harm (especially abuse). This may possibly result from a particular characteristic of the child or his or her family (eg disability, marital conflict) but most often results from the nature of the society within which the disabled child lives (Middleton, 1992). 'Protection' here denotes the safeguarding of the child's physical and psycho-logical well being, with particular reference to the prevention of physical, sexual or emotional abuse or neglect of the child.

The Increased Vulnerability of Disabled Children
A recent review of over twenty studies relating to the abuse of disabled children concluded that children and young people with disabilities were at increased risk for abuse (Westcott, 1991). The review considered a variety of studies which had either attempted

to locate disability amongst abused samples of children, or which had tried to establish prevalence of abuse amongst disabled populations. Although a number of methodological problems beset most of the studies reviewed (see Westcott, 1991), some factors were identified which contributed to the vulnerability of disabled children.

These included dependency upon others for basic and social needs; compliance and obedience 'instilled' as good behaviour; lack of knowledge about sex; isolation and negation by the able-bodied majority increasing responsiveness to attention from others (however inappropriate); difficulties experienced in trying to communicate about abuse, and lack of control or choice experienced by children with disabilities. Many of these issues are discussed in more detail below.

The review also considered the role of society in failing to address—and meet—the needs of children with disabilities. It highlighted the difficulties facing the disabled child who wishes to disclose—perhaps non-verbally—an abusive episode, and the additional problems facing adults in identifying disabled victims. Fundamentally, the review argued that it is society's response to disabled children and adults which increases their vulnerability to abuse. Two typical responses are illustrative: "No one would abuse a *disabled* child—that's just despicable!" or "Well, they're disabled anyway, what will it matter?". Both responses signify the way in which disabled children and adults are perceived as different, second-class citizens in society, and reveal prejudices associated with the marginalisation of disabled people (see, for example, Garbarino, 1987; Middleton, 1992; Sullivan, Vernon & Scanlan, 1987).

Stereotypes of disabled people such as these can result in the failure to provide adequate child protection services for children with disabilities. For example, social workers investigating sexual abuse in one family did not even question the blind sibling of the victim, although she had also been sexually, physically and emotionally abused by the perpetrator (Westcott, 1992). Research in progress at the NSPCC is attempting to gain a better understanding of the issues involved when children (and adults) with disabilities are abused. NSPCC child care professionals working with disabled children have been surveyed about their experiences, and interviews have been conducted with disabled adults who were abused as children (Westcott, 1992). The information obtained from those who have experienced abuse at first hand—both victims and professionals—will play a crucial role in developing appropriate, and more sensitive, child protection services for children with disabilities.

The result of societal segregation of people with disabilities is that disabled children become emotionally and physically dependent upon others for meeting their physical and social needs, and they are prevented from making everyday choices about their lives—control remains with their able bodied peers or carers. Thus, opportunities for abuse are created where disabled children are dependent upon others for the most intimate of activities—washing, dressing, etc., and their disability is used to provide them with few or no resources to defend themselves. For example, disabled children typically receive little or no sex education and are isolated in special schools, so making it increasingly difficult for them to locate or contact possible sources of help (Westcott, 1991).

The whole issue of communication is fundamental to the vulnerability of children and young people with disabilities. From the child's perspective, children with disabilities, and particularly learning difficulties, are much more likely to find it difficult to make a verbal disclosure, so the onus is on those carers and adults with whom they have contact to be aware of the possibility of abuse, and to know what steps need to be taken if they become suspicious. Most child protection agencies and local authorities are ill equipped, for example, to deal with cases involving children who communicate entirely through non-verbal means, and the necessity for dual-specialists (aware of both child protection and disability issues) has been noted (Kennedy, 1990).

Child protection workers have reported finding it more problematic to work with abused children with learning difficulties, trying to find the appropriate level of understanding for the child (Westcott, 1992). Thus, they talk about working with the child at his or her 'functional' age, perhaps using methods they would normally use with a younger child, but simultaneously expressing the wish not to 'baby' the older child with learning difficulties. Appropriate training and development of skills are essential.

Reducing Vulnerability of Disabled Children

A number of measures have been proposed to reduce the vulnerability of children with disabilities (see Sobsey & Mansell, 1990, and Westcott, 1991, for reviews), and these become even more effective if incorporated into the provision of family support. Basically, these measures have the objective of empowering disabled children; similarly, the function of support services can be seen as empowering families.

Empowering Disabled Children and Families

The empowerment of children with disabilities

The disempowerment experienced by disabled children extends

throughout all aspects of their lives, and so empowerment is a crucial step in helping disabled children to protect themselves. Such empowerment is essential regardless of whether the child lives within a family or institutional setting, but *must not be used* to transfer responsibility for the prevention (or occurrence) of abuse on to the child.

For the child with disabilities, empowerment means being afforded choice, wherever possible, over day-to-day decisions affecting his or her life. For example, over choosing which clothes to wear, which food to eat, play friends, school activities, etc. Giving the child the chance to make choices over relatively minor decisions shows him or her that his/her decision making skills are respected, and encourages the child to take part in more major decisions regarding his/her life. It also increases the child's self esteem, and so empowers him or her.

This empowerment can affect other aspects of the disabled child's life. Being given the chance to say 'yes' or 'no' in relatively minor matters can be coupled with appropriate sex education, for example, so that the child is taught to recognise appropriate and inappropriate touching or other behaviours. It is important to emphasise the degree to which disabled children are 'conditioned' to comply with the requests of adults and/or able-bodied peers (otherwise they are viewed as being particularly 'difficult'), so that decision making (in and outside of sex education) must be encouraged repeatedly, and throughout all aspects of their lives in order to have effect.

For disabled children empowerment also means being given equal access to all services and facilities open to their able-bodied peers. Isolation of disabled children in special schools and other residential centres effectively reduces their access to recreational facilities, for example shops, playgrounds, swimming pools, and can lead to break downs in family and peer relationships outside the school. It also makes it increasingly difficult for the child to locate help and identify a trusted person to whom he/she could reveal victimisation (Westcott, 1991). Further, such isolation reduces the child's contact with other adults or peers, and so reduces the possibility of abuse being identified.

It should be noted that the increase in integration of children with disabilities into 'mainstream' activities and services will result in more people with no experience of disability taking a lead role in caring for children with special needs. These adults will need particular guidance about communicating with the child, and concerning behaviours that may be associated with the child's disability. Additionally, they may need extra training on potential indicators of child abuse. Parents will also need assurances about the safety of their children in such settings (Russell, 1992, personal communication).

One pertinent example of the way in which the dis-empowerment of disabled children is linked to their vulnerability to abuse concerns their experiences with the medical profession (Cross, 1990). Disabled adults speak of the way in which their (often frequent) contact with various medical professionals denies them privacy and choice over what happens to their bodies and opens up opportunities for abuse. The very act of being examined is often interpreted as abusive, especially if the child is asked to strip totally naked and submit to examination in front of many students or other professionals.

One disabled woman has spoken of the way in which her frequent hospital visits resulted in her vulnerability to sexual abuse by another member of hospital staff:

> "What the doctors did, they lifted up my nightdress, they poked here and they pushed here without asking me, but in front of a load of other people—it was absolutely no different from the abuse. I didn't say no to any doctor, the porter actually was to me doing absolutely nothing different at all to what every doctor or nurse had ever done." (*Westcott, 1992*)

This example again highlights the relationship between the empowerment of disabled children and the reduction of the vulnerability. Only by treating disabled children equally as their able-bodied peers, and by making adults equally (if not more) responsible for the identification of abuse in disabled children as in able-bodied children, will the problem be appropriately tackled.

The empowerment of families with disabled children: the provision of family support

Dunst, Cooper and Bolick (1987) have defined social support as including:

> "emotional, physical, informational, instrumental, and material assistance provided to others to maintain well-being, promote adaptations to different life events, and foster development in an adaptive manner." (p22)

If this definition is applied to the family with a disabled child, it is possible to identify the role such support may play in reducing the vulnerability of the child with disabilities. The development and maintenance of effective support systems for families with disabled children can have a positive effect on family functioning, and thus decrease the probability of child abuse. Dunst *et al.* (1987) suggest this is through the positive influence that family support has on 'personal well-being, family integrity, parental attitudes toward their child, and parental styles of interaction' (p20). However, it is essential that such support is developed in **partnership** with the parents, and with the child where possible (Authier, 1987; Brimblecombe & Russell, 1988; Russell, 1991).

Dunst *et al.* (1987) have developed a theory of social support which recognises the societal context of abuse—that is the pressure that factors outside of the family can bring to bear upon the family—and which identifies both 'predisposing factors' and 'precipitating events' operating in abusive situations. For the family with a disabled child, such predisposing factors might be the parents' unrealistic expectations of the child, or parental attributions of the intentions underlying the child's behaviour. The precipitating events may include bouts of prolonged child crying, the excessive time demands involved in bringing up a child with disabilities (Authier, 1987; Russell, 1991), or other life crises. Westcott (1991) illustrates the way predisposing factors and precipitating events may interact:

> "Thus parents' expectations of their child may affect whether a child's failure to show affection, for example, results in increased stress and frustration for the parents (and thus possible abuse) or whether it is accepted as the norm." (p252)

Family support 'buffers' the parents from the 'negative reactions often associated with the birth and rearing of a handicapped child' (Dunst *et al.* 1987, p32), and so helps prevent abuse.

Russell (1990) has succinctly described how provision of social support can empower parents of disabled children. The Honeyland's survey of consumer needs revealed that:

> "Parents needed far more specific information about the nature of their child's difficulties and about the available services than was normally provided. Parents wished to have a practical and active participation in caring for their children, but many needed emotional and practical support to exercise such a sole." (p30)

Several key areas in which appropriate family support is crucial have been identified (Russell, 1991); at the time of initial diagnosis, through the provision of counselling for parents and fostering of realistic expectations for their child; recognition of the real difficulties many parents face in bringing up disabled children, and the provision of respite care. Authier (1987) and Russell (1991) note the importance of respect for parents, and of the development of trusting relationships between parents and other professionals. It is also necessary to consider the total family system, recognising the needs of parents and siblings as well as the needs of the child. Informal support networks—friends and other family members—may also have a role to play.

Through the explicit consideration of these and other needs of families with disabled children, support services—health, education and welfare—can be appropriately co-ordinated to meet the needs of the family and child. It is also important to recognise the particular problems facing disabled young people—school leavers who are often unsupported, isolated, lonely and depressed without meaningful daytime occupations (Bryan, 1990; Russell, 1991). This co-ordination of services is essential, if children and young people with disabilities are to be afforded the same protection as able-bodied children and young people; their need for appropriate therapy and counselling services must not be ignored. (Sullivan & Scanlan, 1990, describe their therapeutic programme for abused children with disabilities).

'Honeylands': Co-ordinated Family Support Services for Families with Disabled Children

One notable example of the way in which support services can be provided to families with disabled children is 'Honeylands', a centre based in Devon. The development of Honeylands has been well described elsewhere (Brimblecombe & Russell, 1988; Russell, 1990), and a recent seminar documents (and celebrates) its success (Riches, 1990). The aims of Honeylands are described below; the collaboration of the community health services, social services, education authority, and voluntary organisations has been essential in the achievement of these aims.

> "Family support in the Honeylands context was seen as involving the provision of information for parents about the nature of their child's handicap; helping parents to come to terms with their own feelings about the handicap and teaching them the special skills needed in order to maximise their confidence and competence as parents in helping their child to develop. Intrinsic to this service was the provision of flexible day and short-term residential support as well as guidance at different stages in the child's life in ways appropriate to individual family life-styles. It was felt that Honeylands should be available day or night whenever the family themselves felt they needed advice or relief in order to reduce the strain and exhaustion that came from the continual responsibility for the care of a handicapped child." (Brimblecombe & Russell, 1988, p4).

Honeylands provides baby groups; pre-school playgroups, mothers' groups, family support (residential facilities); clinics; primary health care; home visiting and, essentially, co-ordination with all other services in contact with the family. The involvement of parents in all stages of the development of Honeylands has been of paramount importance; the complementary expertise of both parents and professionals is recognised (Russell, 1990).

It is very easy to see the way in which a centre such as Honeylands can reduce the vulnerability of disabled children, and Brimblecombe and Russell (1988) hint as much:

> "The central resource of Honeylands has clearly met a special need as a 'single door' approach to working with problems in childhood and, in some instances, **to prevention of subsequent handicap**." (*p.25, my emphasis.*)

Vulnerability is reduced through two pathways: on the one hand, the stresses and pressures on parents and carers are reduced, and, on the other hand, more opportunities for early identification and/or 'disclosure' by the child are afforded.

Thus the likelihood of parents and carers abusing their child is reduced, and the child is more frequently in contact with a wide range of trusted adults to whom he/she could disclose. Additionally, the professionals themselves are provided more opportunity to monitor the child and identify any possible signs of abuse.

The communication between different agencies is likely to prevent disabled children (particularly those with learning difficulties) 'falling through the net' or 'between the stools' of different service agencies. This problem—of agencies not taking responsibility for the welfare of children with disabilities—is regularly encountered by social workers working with abused disabled children whose vulnerability is thereby increased (see Martin, 1990; Westcott, 1992).

In a centre such as Honeylands, services are provided according to the needs of the child, rather than other arbitrary criteria. The problems facing young adults with learning difficulties are a case in point: too old to be included under local authority child protection procedures, young adults with learning difficulties remain particularly vulnerable to abuse by others with whom they have contact. In addition, they are regarded as unreliable and/or non-credible witnesses, should they try to bring a case against the perpetrator (Coles, 1990). Although advocacy groups can play an important role in empowering young people with physical disabilities and/or learning difficulties (Bryan, 1990), it is essential that appropriate reporting and therapeutic services are easily accessible and available for any disabled young adult who may have been abused (see Russell, 1991, for a discussion of support services for disabled young people).

The Children Act: Children with Disabilities

The 1989 Children Act introduced a new opportunity to develop appropriate support services for disabled children and their families, and explicitly portrays the need for child protection services to be appropriate and accessible for this group of children (Department of Health, 1991). Russell (1991) provides an excellent summary of the Children Act as it relates to children with disabilities and their families, and Macdonald (1991) explores in more detail the implications of the Act for disabled children from different cultural backgrounds.

Under the Act, work with children with disabilities should be grounded on the following principles:

• The welfare of the child should be safeguarded and promoted by those providing services;

• A primary aim should be to promote access for all children to the same range of services;

• Children with disabilities are children first;

• Recognition of the importance of parents and families in children's lives;

• Partnership between parents and local authorities and other agencies;

• The views of children and parents should be sought and taken into account.

   (*Department of Health, 1991, p2.*)

These principles closely relate to the issues that have been raised earlier in this chapter; for example, equal access to services, and the concept of partnership between parents and professionals. The legislation specifically gives disabled children and their families a voice—a critical step in their empowerment.

The Act makes important requirements of local authorities (and other agencies) which should—if acted upon positively, and given proper resourcing—facilitate the development of appropriate support and child protection services. Specifically, the Act

• Imposes new duties on the SSD towards children **in need** and their families. The definition of children **in need** includes children with disabilities;

- Requires SSDs to provide services designed to minimise the effect of a child's disabilities and to give a child with disabilities the opportunity to lead as normal a life as possible;

- Requires SSDs providing services to give due consideration to the child's religious persuasion, racial origin, cultural and linguistic background;

- Gives SSDs new responsibilities for children it is looking after;

- Provides a range of new court orders to protect children at risk.

(*Department of Health, 1991, p2.*)

The particular vulnerability of disabled children is acknowledged, and the maintenance of a register of all disabled children required—this latter to stimulate appropriate service provision. However, as Macdonald (1991) has pointed out, it is essential that families with disabled children, and the children themselves, are not stigmatised by the process of registration and association with public care. It is also of some considerable concern that the Act introduces the concept of charging for some services provided (for example, respite care, laundry or day care), as families with disabled children typically have lower incomes generally, as well as the additional costs of caring for a child with disabilities (Macdonald, 1991; Russell, 1991).

It is also important that any Guardians ad Litem or Independent Visitors (for children in residential care) who are appointed under the Act be aware of any specific issues relating to the child's disability (and are selected with that in mind). This would include an awareness of the child's preferred mode of communication, and a willingness to ensure that the child's views are actively sought about different issues concerning him or her (as specified in the Act). Such encouragement would offer further opportunities for disabled children to talk about any anxieties they may have (and perhaps 'disclose' abuse); fears have been expressed that many disabled children will not be heard because of misunderstandings that they can not be listened to, and, indeed, have nothing to say (Russell, 1992, personal communication).

Vulnerability and The Need for Protection: Some Conclusions
This chapter has highlighted the particular vulnerability of disabled children, and has discussed the role of family support in reducing that vulnerability. It has briefly described 'Honeylands', an example of how support services can be provided in a co-ordinated and non-stigmatising manner.

The implementation of the Children Act (1989) signals a new way of working with disabled children and their families, but needs proper resourcing and a positive approach in order to succeed. The concept of partnership, between the child, family and professionals, is essential in attempting to achieve the Act's objectives. Significantly, the Act requires the child's 'religiuous persuasion, racial origin and cultural and linguistic background' to be considered. Support services for families from ethnic minority groups have been particularly lacking, and the abuse of disabled children from the different cultural and ethnic communities barely considered (Macdonald, 1991).

Disabled children are at risk from abuse. It is time for society to recognise its responsibilities with respect to this particularly vulnerable group, and to implement appropriate services to support families and children and reduce their vulnerability. Only when this responsibility is acknowledged and acted upon will disabled children become equal, valued members of their communities.

References

Authier, K. J. (1987). The community basis for protecting handicapped children. In J. Garbarino, P. E. Brookhauser & K. J. Authier (Eds), *Special Children—Special Risks: The Maltreatment of Children with Disabilities*. New York: De Gruyter.

Brimblecombe, F. & Russell, P. (1988). *Honeylands: Developing a Service for Families with Handicapped Children*. London: National Children's Bureau.

Bryan, W. (1990). Empowering the Consumer. *Children & Society*, 4(1), 114-119.

Coles, W. (1990). Sexual abuse of persons with disabilities: a law enforcement perspective. *Developmental Disabilities Bulletin*, 18(2), 35-43.

Cross, M. (1990). Perspectives of disability. Paper presented to London Borough of Croydon Seminar, *Abused Children with Disabilities*. Croydon, 9 March.

Department of Health (1991). *The Children Act Guidance and Regulations Volume 6. Children with Disabilities*. London: HMSO.

Dunst, C. J., Cooper, C. S. & Bolick, F. A. (1987). Supporting families of handicapped children. In J. Garbarino, P. E. Brookhauser, K. J. Authier (Eds), *Special Children—Special Risks: The Maltreatment of Children with Disabilities*. New York: De Gruyter.

Garbarino, J. (1987). The abuse and neglect of special children: an introduction to the issues. In J. Garbarino, P. E. Brookhauser & J. Authier (Eds), *Special Children—Special Risks: The Maltreatment of Children with Disabilities*. New York: De Gruyter.

Kennedy, M. (1990). The deaf child who is sexually abused. *Child Abuse Review*, 4(2), 3-6.

Krents, E., Schulman, V. & Brenner, S. (1987). Child abuse and the disabled child: perspectives for parents. *Volta Review*, 89, 78-95.

Macdonald, S. (1991). *All Equal Under the Act? A Practical Guide to the Children Act 1989 for Social Workers*. London: Race Equality Unit (Personal Social Services).

Martin, T. (1990). Whose duty? *Insight*. September 26, 20-21.

Middleton, L. (1992). *Children First: Working with Children and Disability*. Birmingham: Venture Press.

Riches, P. (1990) (Ed). Beyond childhood disability to adult autonomy: a seminar in honour of Professor Frederic Brimblecombe. *Children & Society*, 4(1) (special issue).

Russell, P. (1991). Working with children with physical disabilities and their families—the social work role. In M. Oliver (ed), *Social Work: Disabled People and Disabling Environments*. London: Jessica Kingsley Publishers.

Russell, P. (1990). Honeylands: developing a service for families with children with disabilities and special needs. *Children & Society*, 4(1), 28-34.

Sobsey, D. & Mansell, S. (1990). The prevention of sexual abuse of people with developmental disabilities. *Developmental Disabilities Bulletin*, 18(2), 51-66.

Sullivan, P. M. & Scanlan, J. M. (1990). Psychotherapy with handicapped sexually abused children. *Developmental Disabilities Bulletin*, 18(2), 21-34.

Sullivan, P. M., Vernon, M. & Scanlan, J. M. (1987). Sexual abuse of deaf youth. *American Annals of the Deaf*, 3, 256-262.

Westcott, H. L. (1991a). The abuse of disabled children: a review of the literature. *Child Care, Health and Development*, 17, 243-258.

Westcott, H. L. (1992). *The abuse of children and adults with disabilities*. Report in preparation.

CHAPTER 7

Helping Parents to Manage Children's Sleep Disturbance
An Intervention Trial using Health Professionals

Lyn Quine

Introduction

Sleep disturbance is a widespread form of challenging behaviour, which affects families bringing up both handicapped and non-handicapped children. Many children have disturbed sleeping patterns. Studies have estimated that up to 20 per cent of two-year old children and 14 per cent of three-year old children wake regularly during the night. In the Isle of Wight survey, Rutter and his colleagues (1970) found that even at ten to twelve years old up to 20 per cent of children are regarded by their parents as having problems of this nature. Night-time difficulties are known to be associated with maternal distress and with daytime behavioural difficulties.

Young people with severe learning difficulties seem to be particularly likely to present sleep problems. Bartlet and colleagues (1985), in a study of 214 children with severe learning difficulties under 16 years of age, found that 86 per cent of those under 6 years old, 81 per cent of 6 to 11 year olds, and 77 per cent of the 12 to 16 year olds were reported by parents as having sleep problems: 56 per cent woke on average once a night, 53 per cent had difficulty getting the child to go the bed and 56 per cent in settling the child.

An earlier study by the author (Quine, 1991) found that 51 per cent of a sample of children with severe learning disabilities (aged 0-16) had night settling problems, 67 per cent had night waking problems, and 32 per cent of parents reported that they did not get enough sleep. All three problems were remarkably persistent: of the children who had settling problems, almost half still had problems three years later, while of the children who had waking problems over two-thirds still had them three years later. The children who were most likely to present sleep problems were those with poor communication skills. Mothers of such children showed high levels of stress. They were also more likely to engage in certain behavioural patterns towards their child at night. We called these *maternal responsiveness*. Such mothers were more likely to attend to the child

[101]

immediately at night by offering drinks, cuddles and attention. They were less likely to allow the child to cry for a few minutes, to play music to help settle the child, or to read him/her a bedtime story. We speculated that maternal responsiveness might have the effect of initially encouraging and then maintaining sleep problems, while limited communication skills might make it harder for parents to train such children to present more appropriate bedtime behaviour.

Our next step was to consider methods of treatment for sleep problems. Although widely used, night sedation appears to be of limited value for managing sleep problems in children with severe learning disabilities, and there is some evidence that hypnotic drugs may actually be inappropriate since their use is associated with REM sleep depression, which has been found to be already impoverished in this particular group. However, we had come across a number of studies in the literature that suggested that the use of behavioural approaches offered promise in the management of sleep disturbance, and that parents could be effective teachers of their own children at home. We decided to develop and test a cascade model of training which would make efficient use of scarce professional resources and would recognize the important role of parents as co-therapists and teachers. The approach makes the assumption that parental involvement in therapy will benefit both child and parents, either directly as a result of enhancing parental management, teaching and interactive skills or indirectly by improving family functioning through support and counselling.

Aims of the Study

The aims of the study were twofold: (1) to develop and evaluate a three-day training course for health professionals in the use of behavioural approaches to the management of sleep disturbance, and (2) to set up an intervention trial with 25 families to assess whether training health professionals to teach behavioural techniques to parents is effective in reducing children's sleep disturbance.

Design and Methodology

Evaluating the effectiveness of training health professionals to teach parents behavioural approaches to the management of sleep disturbance was therefore carried out in two stages:

- the development and evaluation of a three-day course in behavioural approaches to sleep disturbance for health professionals.

- an intervention trial in which 12 trained health visitors and community nurses worked with a group of 25 families who had a child with both learning difficulties and sleep disturbance.

Procedures for Organising and Evaluating the Training Course

The study was carried out with the full co-operation and active support of Medway District Health Authority. Twelve health professionals—7 health visitors, 1 community nurse, 2 district nurses and 2 school nurses—from various areas of the health district were seconded to the research team for the course of the study. The anticipation was that the professionals would be relieved of at least part of their normal workload. The selected staff had not had professional contact with any of the families before, so all families started from the same base. The researchers worked closely alongside the health visitors/community nurses, supervising, advising and monitoring the parents' training programme.

Training staff in behavioural approaches to sleep disturbance

The 12 health professionals attended an introductory course on behavioural approaches to sleep disturbance which was held one day a week for three weeks at the University. The course was staggered for two reasons: firstly to facilitate assimilation and learning and secondly for practical purposes, since it was difficult for professionals to be absent from their normal work for three full days in one week. A further day was convened one week after the end of the course for the details of the intervention trial to be discussed and the research materials and sleep diaries handed out. The course was taught by an educational and a social psychologist, both of whom were qualified teachers, and a clinical psychologist. The role playing sessions were organised by a lecturer in social work, who used role-play routinely in teaching social work practice.

After a short introduction to the principles of behavioural theory, the techniques were introduced in sequence so that it was possible to underpin each technique with the minimum necessary theory both in the seminar discussion and in take-home notes written specially for the purpose. The first day of the course (Unit 1) was concerned with teaching behavioural principles and considering their application to the management of sleep disturbance. The main techniques that can be used to change sleep behaviour were then introduced. Each teaching session was followed by group exercises during which group members were able to test their understanding of the principles and techniques against examples from their own experience and from case histories of children with sleep disturbance.

The second day of the course (Units 2 and 3) was concerned with teaching health professionals how to take a history of the sleep problem and how to identify the extent and severity of the problem behaviour and the factors that appear to maintain it. The health professionals also learned how to teach parents to observe and record sleep behaviour accurately by means of a sleep diary, how to identify goals for treatment, how to break them into steps for teaching and how to set up a management plan (*see Figure 1*).

Figure 1

Setting up a Management Plan

First Session

1. Both parents to attend first session.
2. Gather information about parents' concerns.
3. Take a history.
4. Help parents identify the problem behaviour.
5. Identify parents' preferred outcome.
6. Teach parents to use a sleep diary.

Second Session

1. Explain what the programme is about and obtain informed consent.
2. Teach parents to analyse behaviour in terms of ABC pattern.
3. Identify the antecedents of the child's behaviour.
4. Identify the consequences of the child's behaviour.
5. Teach parents techniques and discuss management options.
6. Help parents choose a management strategy.
7. Identify useful reinforcers (rewards).
8. Help to plan steps of chosen strategy, pin-point pitfalls.
9. Weekly visits to advise and check on progress using diary to look for change in child's behaviour.

The third day (Unit 4) was devoted entirely to practising interview techniques and role-playing how to teach the principal behavioural techniques to parents. We saw this as a particularly important component of the course, since it was essential to establish that the health professionals were able not only to learn the behavioural approach to managing sleep problems for themselves but also to teach it to parents. The role players, who had experience of children with severe learning difficulties, were briefed beforehand using details from actual case studies from our records. The practice sessions were video-recorded and discussed at the end of the session.

During the course the health professionals built up a personal reference manual. Each professional was given a hard backed ring binder containing transparent envelopes. For each component of the course or group activity a card containing the main points of teaching and space for notes, comments and answers was provided which could be slipped into one of the plastic envelopes. In addition, for the purposes of the evaluation, health professionals were supplied with standard format interview schedules for carrying out the initial behavioural interview with parents, progress assessment sheets, sleep diaries and sleep management contract forms on which the agreed sleep programme could be summarised and signed by parents and health professionals.

The course was evaluated by administration of a pre and post course test of Knowledge of Behavioural Priniciples as Applied to Children (KBPAC: O'Dell, Tarler-Benlolo and Flynn, 1979). All the health professionals significantly improved in their knowledge of behavioural principles during the course. The mean knowledge score was 25.8 (s.d. 7.0) at Time 1 and 37.0 (s.d. 6.6) at Time 2 (t=7.8, d.f. = 11, p <0.001).

Procedures for Organising and Evaluating the Intervention Trial

Sample selection

The intervention trial took place in the Medway health district. All the Medway schools, social education centres, and child assessment and care centres that ran playgroups for pre-school children with learning difficulties were approached and asked to send a letter home to parents (examples of all documentation can be found in Quine and Wade, 1991). The letter contained details of the study and offered places on the programme to parents. Forty families initially expressed interest in taking part in the study, and 25 families (63 per cent) completed programmes. These families formed the experimental group. All fulfilled the criteria we had selected for eligibility for inclusion in the study. These were one of the following: night settling problems—usually three or more times a week; night waking—usually three or more times a week; limited hours' sleep—usually three or more times a week. Figure 2 shows the dropout from the study.

The children who finally received treatment were quite a highly selected group. It is quite possible that there was a bias in the families who expressed interest, and of those, 65 per cent entered treatment. This compares with 50 per cent in the study of non-handicapped children by Richman, Douglas, Hunt, Lansdown and Levere (1985). Although our previous studies found no sex differences in the prevalence of sleep problems, almost twice as many boys as girls entered the programme. In addition, there was considerable marital unhappiness and maternal irritability in the treatment group. It is interesting to speculate whether factors relating to marital unhappiness and maternal irritability were influential in the parents' decision to seek treatment for the child.

Figure 2

Dropout from Study

40 families expressed interest

- 25 (63%) completed programmes
- 1 dropped out during programme
- 14 dropped out before intervention began
  - 3 had family problems
  - 1 child went into residential care
  - 1 child went into phased care
  - 1 child went into foster care
  - 2 felt programme offered would not help
  - 1 failed to keep initial appointment and to respond to further letters
  - 5 no longer had a sleep problem

Design

A single-case experimental design with multiple baseline across subjects was chosen. In this type of study, by convention, the letter A is used to designate a baseline (no treatment) condition, the letter B to designate treatment. In the A/B design, the initial period of observation involves the repeated measurement of the natural frequency of occurrence of the target behaviour under study. This period is defined as the baseline, or A phase, of the study. The primary purpose of baseline measurement is to have a standard against which to evaluate the effectiveness of the subsequent experimental intervention. The B phase of the study is the introduction of treatment. A treatment effect is demonstrated by showing that performance differs from one phase to the next. In a multiple baseline across subjects, a treatment is applied *in sequence* to a single targeted behaviour across a number of subjects exposed to similar environmental conditions. Baseline measurements continue to be collected for the rest of the group. The controlling effect of the treatment is inferred from the rate change in the treated subject(s) against their own baseline and against the rate for the (as yet) untreated subjects in the group—who should remain unchanged.

Teaching parents the techniques

An initial visit by the health professionals to each of the families in the experimental group took place. At this meeting the sleeping problem was clearly specified, and parents were asked to keep baseline recordings of their son or daughter's sleeping patterns for a two-week period using a sleep diary. A sleep diary provides an accurate record of the child's sleep patterns and provides feedback to both parents and health professional about the initial severity of the problem and the progress the child is making. Difficulty in settling to sleep, frequency and duration of episodes of night waking, sleeping in the parents' bed and repeated coming downstairs were recorded. Background information about the management techniques parents had already tried, the child's behaviour, and mental and physical impairments were also collected. The child's doctor was consulted to confirm that there were no medical reasons why a sleep management programme should not be implemented. On the second visit, a week later, the baseline data were examined, and a treatment/training programme tailored to individual family needs was negotiated with the parents and young person (where possible). This was written up on a chart, and the parents were requested to continue recording the child's sleep patterns in the diary throughout the trial.

Four techniques were taught. The first involved setting the scene for the desired behaviour or introducing *positive routines*. Many children with sleep problems do not have a regular bedtime routine, so they do not associate going to bed with going to sleep. The routine should last about half an hour and should involve such things as washing or bathing the child, a drink and a biscuit, preparation for bed, a cuddle and a bedtime story. This provides the child with a clear, unequivocal cue that bedtime is approaching. The child should then be settled in bed and left to sleep.

Some children have learned to associate going to sleep with being rocked, or with the parent lying down in their bed with them. If they wake up in the night and they are not being rocked, or the parent is absent, they are unable to go back to sleep. Parents can teach the child to associate dropping off to sleep with a variety of cues such as a cuddly toy, or soft music from a cassette player, instead of their parent's presence.

The second technique involves removing incentives for sleep disturbance by not attending to the child when he or she cries or makes a fuss. The child has learned that his/her difficult behaviour produces rewards in the form of cuddles, attention or the postponement of bedtime. This method is called extinction, and can achieve dramatic results in a short time. However, it involves leaving the child to cry and many parents find this very stressful. The method usually results in an initial increase in frequency and intensity of the problem behaviour, and so its use is only to be recommended for parents who feel strong enough to cope with this or those who require very quick results. It should never be used if the child is unwell.

The third technique is a variation of extinction and is much easier to use. It involves a step by step approach to the problem. Instead of leaving the child to cry, the parent gradually distances herself from the child's room. First she sits by the bed, holding the child's hand or stroking him. Then when the child settles without fuss, she gradually moves her chair step by step from the room on subsequent evenings until she sits first by the door, and then outside the room. During these steps she should have as little interaction as possible with her child. Eventually when the child settles quickly the mother no longer needs to sit by the bedroom door but can enjoy her evening.

A variation of the graded steps approach can be used for the child who wakes in the night. The parent should wait for a few minutes longer each night before she goes to the child. Eventually the child will learn that his crying is not being rewarded and will stop making a fuss when he wakes.

The final techique that was taught is called positive reinforcement, and can be used in conjunction with the other techniques. It involves rewarding the child for appropriate night-time behaviour. The parent can use a star chart where the child is rewarded with a gold star if he stays in his bed or sleeps throughout the night without disturbing his parents. When a number of stars has been collected, these can be exchanged for a small toy. Reinforcers can be anything the child enjoys, such as praise, sweets or toys. One child we worked with enjoyed a musical light show toy and this was used as an effective reinforcer. There are three vital rules governing the use of reinforcement: (1) A reward should never be taken away once it has been earned. (2) The child should be able to earn a reward easily at the beginning so that he can experience success. Later on the requirements for earning a reward can be increased. (3) Parents' praise is the main force behind the effectiveness of the reward. Rewards can be faded when the desired behaviour is established.

Parents were advised to avoid prolonged routines and overstimulation, and were taught about the importance of being consistent in their approach. They were warned that their progress might initially be slow. Progress was monitored on a regular weekly basis by the health visitor. Frequency of initial home visiting was agreed between parent and health visitor.

Parents were asked to stop recording when the young person settled off easily to sleep and no longer woke at night, or when the parents' sleep was less disrupted, or when an outcome they regarded as satisfactory was reached. Advice on maintaining the improvement was then given. Follow-up took place after three months to check that progress had been maintained.

Although the techniques were relatively straightforward, a range of modifications to the programmes were necessary to suit individual parenting styles and family coping resources. Some parents were extremely reluctant to consider alternatives to well-established but unconstructive coping strategies which were sometimes having the effect of maintaining the sleep problem. Such cases required tact and sensitivity on the part of the health visitor and a degree of flexibility in the techniques to be applied.

Evaluating the effectiveness of the intervention

The study resolves into four questions: Can staff without previous training be taught behavioural approaches to managing sleeplessness? Can parents learn the techniques? Do the techiques work? Do other changes in maternal attitudes and behaviour occur? Appropriate checks were built into the study at each level. They included a test of knowledge of behavioural principles to health visitors; a questionnaire about the programme; a short test for parents to establish how well they had understood the procedures, and data on the success and maintenance of the treatment outcome. After three months we carried out a follow-up in which parents were requested to fill in a two-week diary so that we could check that progress had been maintained.

We hypothesised that if the intervention was successful and the children's sleep patterns improved, other changes might occur within the family. These were most likely to be in the child's daytime behaviour, and also in the mother's responsiveness and her perceptions of herself, her child and her partner. Accordingly, mothers in the experimental group were interviewed before and after the intervention. Measures of maternal stress, maternal responsiveness, attitudes and behaviour, and satisfaction with settling and waking patterns, were taken and the pre and post intervention means were compared by use of matched paired t-test.

Findings

Description of the Treatment Group

The treatment group consisted of 25 children, 17 (68 per cent) of whom were boys and 8 (32 per cent) girls. Eight children (32 per cent) were the only child, 6 (24 per cent) the eldest child, 3 (12 per cent) the middle child and 8 (32 per cent) the youngest child of the family. Twenty-two (88 per cent) came from two parent families and 3 (12 per cent) from single parent families. One child was adopted, but the rest lived with at least one natural parent. Twenty-two mothers (88 per cent) were married, and 1 mother (4 per cent) was divorced, 1 (4 per cent) separated and 1 (4 per cent) single. Eight mothers (32 per cent) had full or part time paid employment. Twenty fathers (80 per cent) were employed and 2 (8 per cent) were unemployed.

The children's skills, abilities and behaviour were assessed using the Behaviour Problem Index (Cunningham et al, 1986). The Behaviour Problem Index is a structured interview designed to elicit from parents and care staff details of the child's physical and development skills, communication skills, sensory impairments, medical conditions and behaviour problems.

Table 1 shows the children's skills and abilities. Over three-quarters of children were mobile, about 40 per cent were continent during the day, about half could feed themselves without help. Three children (12 per cent) had poor vision and 7 (28 per cent) poor hearing. About half had poor understanding and use of communication.

Table 1
Characteristics of Sample

Mobile	19 (76%)
Not mobile	6 (24%)
Continence During Day	
Does not wet	10 (40%)
Does not soil	11 (44%)
Can feed self without help	13 (52%)
Can wash self without help	3 (12%)
Can dress self without help	2 (8%)
Vision Poor or blind	3 (12%)
Hearing Poor or deaf	7 (28%)
Understanding communication	
Poor	14 (56%)
Fair	5 (20%)
Good	3 (12%)
Using Communication	
Poor	12 (48%)
Fair	6 (24%)
Good	3 (12%)

Improvement in Parental Knowledge of Behavioural Principles
In order to test whether the parents had been able to learn the principles of behavioural management, we gave them a short test before and after the intervention. We used a shortened version of the Knowledge of Behavioural Principles as Applied to Children test

(KBPAC) (O'Dell et al, 1979). This is a ten-item test of knowledge. There was a significant improvement between the pre and post test means in the parents' knowledge scores, confirmed by a matched paired t-test. (Time 1 3.8 (s.d. 2.5); Time 2 6.0 (s.d. 2.0)). This shows clearly that parents had learned principles of behavioural management.

Improvement in Sleep Patterns
The results of the treatment programmes were remarkably clear-cut. *All* the children improved in their settling and waking patterns. The Appendix presents some examples. We have shown the child's 'main' problems on each chart, though some children had more than two problems—ie waking frequency, waking duration and sleeping in the parents' bed. Names have been changed to preserve anonymity.

The improvement in the children's *settling* problems was marked. Table 2 presents a summary of the progress of the 15 children with settling problems. It can be seen that the children took from 45 to 180 minutes (mean 111 minutes) to settle to sleep before the intervention, and between 5 and 60 minutes (mean 20.4) to settle after the intervention.

Table 2
Settling Problems: Summary Table

	Time taken to settle at night (average minutes per night)		
	Baseline	Post-Treatment	Improvement
Mark	180	5	175
Laura†	150	56	96
Katy	140	5	135
William	140	10	130
Timothy*	130	10	120
Judith	120	45	75
Patrick*	120	5	115
Robert	120	60	60
Stephen†	120	10	110
Peter	100	25	75
Lucy	95	25	70
Simon	75	10	65
Ben	70	5	65
Mary†	70	25	45
Jonathan	45	10	35

* Falls asleep downstairs.
† Repeatedly comes downstairs.

The children's *waking* patterns improved dramatically too. Table 3 presents a summary of the progress of the 15 children with waking problems. We have calculated both the number of times per night the child woke (awake frequency) and the mean minutes per night the child was awake (awake duration). This allows us to take account of both the child who wakes infrequently but for a long time each waking, and the child who wakes frequently for a short time. Frequently, too, children did not sleep in their own beds at night, choosing either to sleep in the parents' bed, to bed-hop between parent, relative or sibling, or to exchange beds with one parent at some time during the night. The table shows that before the intervention the average number of times per night the children woke up ranged from 2.2 to 4.0 times (mean 3.1), and the average duration of time awake ranged from 30 to 120 minutes (mean 70.2 minutes). After the intervention the average number of wakings per night was from 0 to 1.3 (mean 0.3) and the average duration per night of time awake was from 0 to 15 minutes (mean 3.2).

Table 3
Waking Problems: Summary Table

	Awake Frequency (per night)		Awake Duration (per night)		Does not sleep in own bed (per week)	
	Pre	Post	Pre	Post	Pre	Post
Adam	4	1.3	–	–	5	0
Anthony*	3	0.3	27	5	–	–
Ben	3.5	1	60	5	–	–
Christopher	2.5	0.5	110	5	7	0
Edward	4	0	–	–	5	0
Jane	2.7	0	90	0	–	–
Jenny*	2.5	0	120	0	–	–
Jonathan	2.6	0.4	–	–	6	0
Katy	3	0	–	–	4	0
Martin	2.2	0	50	0	–	–
Matthew	3.5	0	50	0	6	0
Peter	3	0	90	0	–	–
Robert	3	1	–	–	6	1
Ryan	3	0	30	2	6	0
Simon	3	0.3	75	15	–	–

*Mother lies down with child.

Parents were asked to stop recording when the child settled off easily to sleep and no longer woke at night, or when the parents' sleep was less disrupted, or when an outcome that they regarded as satisfactory was reached. The health professionals worked towards goals that had been agreed with parents. Parents varied in their beliefs about what was a suitable bedtime or settling time for their child and this is reflected in the results. Some parents were quite happy for a child to take half an hour or so to settle as long as the child was reasonably quiet and stayed in his or her own bed, leaving the parents to enjoy their evening. At the end of the intervention one or two children, such as Laura and Robert, still took quite a long time to settle to sleep, but Laura had stopped coming downstairs repeatedly and began to settle without fuss, and Robert, a severely physically handicapped child, learned to settle in his own bed at a reasonable bedtime every night.

Each child was given a 'clinical' rating by the two research psychologists. A rating of 1 indicated slight improvement, 2 indicated moderate improvement, 3 indicated marked improvement and 4 indicated that the target for settling or waking had been reached. The ratings were made on the basis of detailed knowledge of each of the cases, scrutiny of the sleep diaries, and information provided by the health visitors. Agreement between the two psychologists was 23/25 (92 per cent). Thus calculated, the overall success rate (those with complete or marked improvement) was 80 per cent. This compares favourably with the success rates reported by other researchers, suggesting that it is possible to achieve similar improvement in children with severe learning difficulties and physical handicaps as in non-handicapped children, and by using trained health professionals instead of experienced clinical psychologists.

Maternal Satisfaction with Settling and Waking Patterns

Most mothers were delighted with the results of the intervention. Mothers were asked to rate their satisfaction with the child's settling and waking patterns on a seven point scale from '1' not satisfied to '7' satisfied. Figures 3 and 4 show that there was a significant difference between the pre and post intervention maternal satisfaction scores for both settling and waking patterns. Only one mother was not satisfied with her child's current settling pattern, and this was a mother who had chosen to implement programmes for settling and waking separately and had not yet moved on to a settling programme. Only one mother was not satisfied with the child's current waking pattern, and for the same reason: the waking programme was to be implemented after the programme for settling. These programmes are now under way. Lucy's mother was neither satisfied nor dissatisfied with her child's settling patterns. The health visitor had worked on her settling patterns, which improved greatly during the programme. However, by the time of the post-intervention interview, Lucy had spent a period of time in hospital. When she came home her behaviour had deteriorated, and she

Figure 3

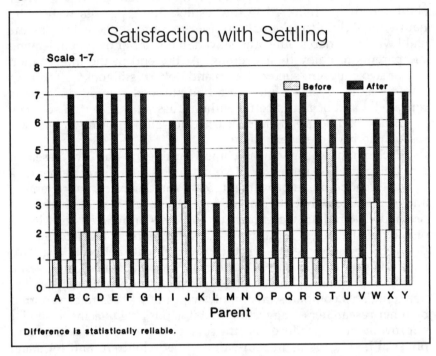

developed a waking problem and began to demand attention during the night. She was referred back to the health visitor.

Many parents commented on their experience with the programmes, the difficulties they had had in implementing them and the usefulness of health visitor support and advice during the intervention. We present a representative selection of their comments below.

- **Anthony's mother**   I was happy with the whole programme and with Margaret's suggestions. At the beginning we didn't like walking out on Anthony, leaving him whimpering. But he stopped. It worked very quickly. He actually enjoys going to bed now.

- **Jonathan's mother**   I knew it was going to be hard because I hate to hear Jonathan cry. At one point in the programme it was suggested that we ignore him altogether, but we couldn't. When we agreed that instead we would just go to him and put him back in bed with minimal interaction we got on much better. It was difficult to stop the naps initially.

Figure 4

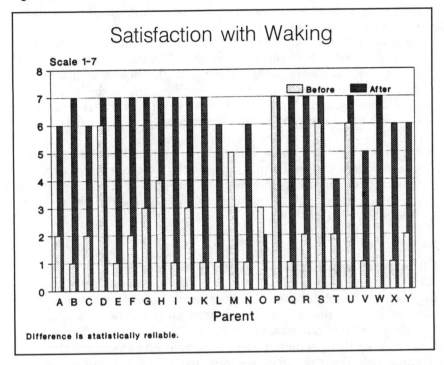

The way the programme was done in steps was excellent. We're really delighted. It was really interesting to write down what was happening and then to be able to *see* how much improvement had been made. Just having the support helps to keep up the programme.

- **Katy's mother** It was difficult to become consistent and disciplined at the beginning, but I realise that becoming consistent myself was what made the programme work. Sticking to the programme was good. Once I could see the benefits, it became so easy. I needed someone to point out to me that I wasn't giving Katy a proper routine. Once I did, it all fell into place.

  It's had repercussions in daytime behaviour. I began to realise that I was letting her lead and not giving her enough guidance. Now I'm more positive with her.

  Night-times are now a real pleasure. I've got nothing but praise for the programme.

- **Ryan's mother** What worked was learning not to respond to Ryan when he woke during the night. The most difficult part was in the second stage when we just had to put him back to bed and leave the room. He kept getting out of bed. I just kept putting him back and leaving the room without saying anything. This happened five or six sometimes and it took about three to four weeks to achieve our goal. I used to give him a few sweets after breakfast and tell him he was a good boy. I think he understands.

Persevering was difficult because I couldn't see how you could make someone sleep longer. But the health visitor was a great support. Once I got into a routine with it, there were no problems. Ryan no longer has temper tantrums. He is much less restless; his concentration has improved.

- **Stephen's mother** The whole programme was easy enough. The health visitor was brilliant. I suppose the pressure to be *consistent* was difficult at the beginning. At the end of the day I guess parents have to look at themselves and change *their* behaviour. That's always difficult.

Changes in the Children's Daytime Behaviour

As we mentioned earlier, we wanted to investigate whether improving the children's sleep patterns would result in other changes too—particularly to the children's daytime behaviour and to the mothers' behaviour and attitudes towards their children. In order to investigate whether there was an improvement in ratings of daytime behaviour we used the Behaviour Problem Index (BPI) to assess the child's behaviour before and after the intervention. For the BPI, 20 items of behaviour are rated 0, 1 or 2 points by the interviewer, who uses objective descriptions of behaviour from parents. A score of 0 signifies no or trivial difficulties, a score of 1 signifies mild difficulties, and a score of 2 signifies marked difficulties. Scores for all items are summed to produce a total score. In order to consider daytime behaviour only we omitted the items realting to night-time difficulties. Figure 5 shows that there were significant differences between the children's pre and post intervention scores on the Behaviour Problem Index, indicating that ratings of the children's daytime behaviour had improved. (Time 1 13.0 (s.d. 4.6); Time 2 9.7 (s.d. 4.3)).

There are three possible explanations for these findings. The first is that once the parents' sleep was less disrupted and they felt less stressed, they began to have a less gloomy view of their child's behavioural difficulties. The second explanation is that the children's behaviour did improve, because they were now getting more sleep. This alone made them more able to concentrate, easier to handle, less likely to have arguments with brothers and sisters, and less fractious and bad-tempered. The third explanation is that the parents were able to generalise their new learning and to apply the behavioural techniques to the management of difficult daytime

Figure 5

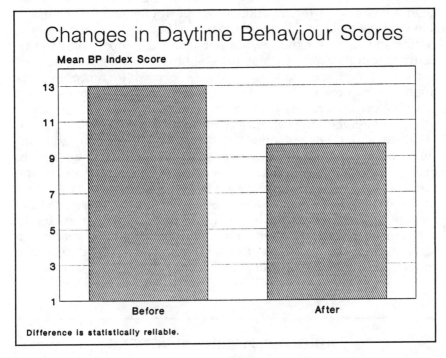

Changes in Daytime Behaviour Scores

Mean BP Index Score

Difference is statistically reliable.

behaviour also, which led to an improvement.It is not possible to tell whether one or all of these explanations is relevant here.

Positive changes in the daytime behaviour of children whose parents were taught behavioural techniques for managing sleep problems have been reported in studies other than ours. Seymour et al (1983) reported that children were described as happier, easier to handle, less aggressive, less grizzly and more settled.

Changes in Maternal Behaviour
Maternal responsiveness
In an earlier study (Quine and Wade, 1991, p. 13) we produced a maternal responsiveness scale incorporating some of the tenets of the behavioural approach, which showed that mothers of children with sleep problems were more likely than other mothers to respond immediately to the child who wakes or refuses to settle to sleep by offering drinks, cuddles and attention, and less likely to allow the child to cry for a few minutes, to play music to help the child settle, or to read the child a bedtime story. The behavioural approach to managing sleep disturbance emphasises the importance of encouraging appropriate behaviours (settling easily to sleep) by attending to or rewarding them, and discouraging problematic bedtime behaviours (refusal to go to bed, repeated coming

downstairs) by withholding the reinforcer that is maintaining the child's behaviour (eg cuddles, the postponement of bedtime, allowing the child to sleep in the parents' bed). Also emphasised is setting the scene for the desired behaviour (by providing positive bedtime routines) and teaching the child to relax to a given stimulus such as a bedtime story or music. We tried to represent this approach in our scale of maternal behaviours. Now we investigated whether there were any changes in maternal rsponsiveness scores after the intervention trial. Each item was scored from '0' never to '4' always. Figure 6 shows that there were indeed significant differences in pre and post intervention scores: mothers were more able to ignore inappropriate behaviour and more able to set the scene for and reinforce appropriate bedtime behaviours by the end of the trial. These changes are, we believe, crucial to behavioural change in the child since they indicate that the parent is able to extinguish episodes of difficult bedtime behaviour by ceasing to reward them and also to provide both cues and rewards for improved bedtime behaviour.

Figure 6

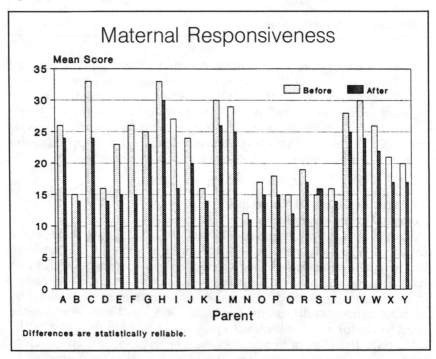

We believe that maternal responsiveness is most usefully viewed as a maintaining factor. This would be consistent with a view that sleep problems are a *learned habit*. Parents of children with mental and physical handicaps are often particularly anxious and concerned about the child, and this may lead them to change their usual patterns of child-rearing. These changes may result in the inadvertent encouragement of undesired bedtime behaviour. If, for example, the parents check on the child immediately at night whenever there is the slightest noise, or allow the child to share their bed, the child will be slow to learn that night-time is a time for sleeping. In addition, the child will soon learn to 'punish' the parents by crying if they do not go in to her or do not allow her into their bed. This quickly weakens the parents' decision to ignore her.

Irritability and smacking
At the end of the intervention mothers reported less irritability with their children. They also smacked their children less frequently and were less afraid of losing control and punishing their child too severely. The differences in pre and post intervention scores were all statistically significant. This is an important finding since it suggests that behavioural training may be a feasible approach to the prevention of parenting difficulties and, perhaps, child abuse.

Changes in Maternal Attitudes
Maternal stress and morale
The results of our earlier study (Quine and Wade, 1991, p. 27) showed that mothers of children with sleep problems had higher levels of stress as measured by the Malaise Inventory than mothers of children without sleep problems. The mean stress score of mothers with settling and waking problems and for those whose child slept regularly in their bed was in each case higher than 6.0.

Michael Rutter and his colleagues (1970), who adapted the Inventory from the Cornell Medical Index, considered scores of 5 or 6 to be outside the normal range and indicative of psychological distress, while scores of 7 or more were 'critical'. The mothers who took part in our intervention trial had a mean score of 6.4 at the start of the trial, indicating considerable psychological distress. However, as Figure 7 shows, there were significant differences between pre and post intervention scores: mothers had become much less stressed by the end of the intervention trial.

Figure 7 also shows that mothers' morale, as measured by Cantrill's Ladder (Cantrill, 1965) had significantly improved. It is well known that mothers caring for children with severe learning difficulties are a group with generally high stress levels and low morale (Quine, 1991), but so far there has been little empirical study of the factors that might improve mothers' psychological health. We

Figure 7

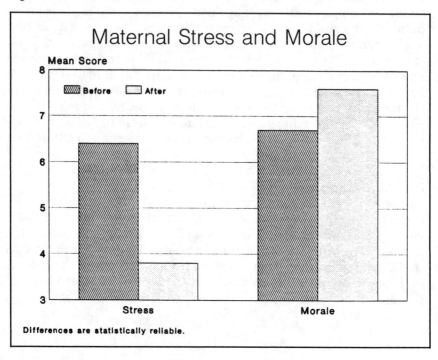

Maternal Stress and Morale

Differences are statistically reliable.

are now able to suggest that teaching parents to manage difficult and challenging behaviour may be one practical solution.

Mother's perceptions of self, child and partner

Given our early argument concerning the value of intervention for family adaptation (p. 102), we wanted to explore possible changes in the attitudes of mothers in our experimental group towards family relationships. We therefore used a number of rating scales to explore the mother's perceptions of herself, her child and her relationship with her partner. These were sets of bi-polar items separated by seven point scales which we adapted from the work of Davis, Booth and Rushton (1988). The value of seven refers to the pole described in the table.

There were 20 items describing the mother's feelings about herself. These were summed to form a total score of positiveness. There was a significant difference between pre and post intervention means, indicating that mothers had a more favourable view of themselves at the end of the intervention. A number of individual items contributed to the change. Mothers felt themselves to be more affectionate, flexible, in control, patient, understanding, happy, competent, relaxed, energetic, good-humoured and confident. They felt less irritable, lonely and depressed. This suggests that involvement in the children's sleep programmes had quite far-reaching effects, not only achieving improvement in the children but also enhancing the mothers' perceptions of self. This might make mothers more able to cope with the care of the handicapped child, and less likely to succumb to the effects of stress. This is particularly important since it is well known that mothers caring for a handicapped child are particularly vulnerable to stress (Quine and Pahl, 1985).

There were 14 items describing the mother's perceptions of her child. These were summed to produce a total score of positiveness. Mothers had developed a much more favourable view of the child by the end of the intervention: they viewed the child as happier, having less of a temper, having better concentration, being more able to manage alone and to communicate needs, being more interested in his or her surroundings, more affectionate, more obedient and more easy to handle.

There were 16 items describing the mother's feelings for her partner. Again there were significant differences between pre and post intervention scores. By the end of the intervention mothers had a more positive view of their feelings about their partner. They saw themselves as more loving and affectionate and happier towards them, spending more time talking to them and being able to confide in them, more able to understand them, more helpful and more joyful towards them. They felt more relaxed with them and less critical.

Three Month Follow-up

Three months after each child's programme was completed, we asked mothers to fill in a two-week sleep diary to check whether progress had been maintained. Two families had not completed the three month period, and three families have so far not responded to requests to fill in sleep diaries, so these results are based on 20 families. Of the 12 children with settling problems, all but one had maintained the progress made, and some had improved upon it. Stephen was now taking about 40 minutes to settle, but this was not a problem for his mother since he now played quietly in his bedroom without disturbing the family. His mother thought that it was a great improvement on the two hours of noisy behavour she had been used to.

Ten out of twelve children had maintained their progress with waking patterns. Simon and Robert's waking patterns seemed to have deteriorated slightly since the final two weeks of the programme. Simon is a multiply handicapped child who had had very severe settling and waking problems accompanied by severe headbanging. Now, although he wakes, his parents are able to check on him and go straight back to bed. His headbanging has decreased dramatically and his mother is satisfied that the improvement in his behaviour has been maintained. Robert is also multiply handicapped. His mother found it very hard to be consistent in her approach to his sleep problems. She was not well herself, and her husband is being treated for depression. Both she and her husband are very anxious about Robert and this sometimes leads her to be very responsive to his cries and demands for attention. However, there has beeen a dramatic improvement in his sleeping patterns overall, as examination of the baseline rates of sleep problems documented in his diary shows. All the children now slept in their own beds through the night.

Overall, 17/20 children (85 per cent) had maintained progress or improved, while Robert and Simon had maintained their progress with settling but had deteriorated slightly from the last two weeks of the programme, and Stephen now took a little longer to settle but no longer came downstairs. However, even these children's sleeping patterns had improved dramatically from their baseline positions.

Conclusions

The purpose of the study was to determine whether health professionals such as health visitors and community nurses could learn and apply behavioural techniques to help parents manage their children's sleep disturbance. The study showed that health visitors and community nurses improved their knowledge of behavioural principles during training. Parents, too, improved in their knowledge after being taught by health professionals. This indicates that the training course was successful in training health professionals in behavioural principles, and that they in turn were able to pass on their knowledge to parents.

The effect of the behavioural treatment was assessed by use of a single case experimental design with multiple baseline across subjects. We were able to demonstrate clearly that while the baselines showing the frequency of occurrence of sleep problems of children treated sequentially improved, the baselines of children awaiting treatment remained relatively stable. This was true for all 25 children in the treatment group. These improvements were, by and large, maintained at three month follow-up. In addition we were able to show that parental satisfaction with their child's settling and waking patterns improved significantly during the course of the intervention.

Clinical ratings of improvement by the research psychologists showed that 80 per cent (20/25) had either reached the target set at the outset of the programme or displayed a marked improvement, 16 per cent (4) showed a moderate improvement and 4 per cent (1) a slight improvement. All children showed some improvement. This success rate compares favourably with the rates reported by other researchers. Richman et al (1985), for example, report a 77 per cent rate of success, measured similarly, while Jones and Verduyn (1983) reported success in 84 per cent of cases, and Seymour et al (1983) in 78 per cent. Each of these studies were carried out with non-handicapped children and used experienced clinical psychologists or child psychiatrists as therapists. These professionals worked with parents who were sufficiently motivated to attend a series of clinic appointments. The success of our study, which used a home-based service, and trained health visitors how to teach behavioural techniques to parents of children with severe learning difficulties who often have additional physical handicaps, suggests that nothing is lost by using such a cascade model of training. There is much to be gained. The cascade model of training allows service managers to make efficient use of scarce specialised professional resources. It allows important skills to be acquired by larger groups of health and social services professionals and to be passed on to parents within a partnership that enhances parental management and interactive and teaching skills, and leads to greater family adaptation and stablity.

Children with severe learning difficulties often have limited use and understanding of language and learn at a much slower rate than do their non-handicapped peers. The greater the learning difficulties the longer the child takes to learn. Physical impairments will add to the difficulty by reducing the opportunities for learning. They can also increase the likelihood that a child will have a sleep problem. Such children often find it difficult to get comfortable at night or find it hard to change position; they may experience discomfort due to muscle spasm; they may be made uncomfortable by incontinence or by skin irritations. Children with visual or hearing impairments may not receive the cues that other children receive that bedtime is approaching. This makes the child with learning difficulties or physical impairment both more prone to sleep disturbance and more difficult to teach. Many children with severe learning difficulties also suffer from epilepsy, and this in itself can disrupt the child's sleeping patterns.

The high success rate in this study shows that behavioural methods of managing night-time disturbance can be effective even with the most difficult children. They are particularly valuable because they do not rely on the child's understanding of language. The child with severe learning difficulties may fail to respond not because s/he cannot but because s/he does not understand what we want him or her to do. Behavioural approaches help parents sort out and simplify the messages given to the child so that he or she has a better chance of understanding. They provide a more constructive alternative to night sedation, which has been, until recently, the most widespread method of dealing with childhood sleep problems.

Overall, then, the study has produced a remarkably clear-cut set of results, showing that it is possible radically to improve children's sleep behaviour, and that the improvements result in a number of positive changes in relationships within the family.

References

Bartlet, L. B., Rooney V. and Spedding, S (1985), Nocturnal difficulties in a population of mentally handicapped children, *British Journal of Mental Subnormality*, 31, 54-59.

Cantrill, H. (1965), *The Pattern of Human Concerns*, Chicago, Rutgers University Press.

Cunningham C., Sloper, T., Rangecroft, A., Knussen, C., Lennings, C., Dixon I. and Reeves, D. (1986), *The Effects of Early Intervention on the Occurrence and Nature of Behaviour Problems in Children with Down's Syndrome*, Final Report to DHSS, Hester Adrian Research Centre, University of Manchester.

Davis H., Booth A. and Rushton R. (1988), Parent counselling and support, Paper presented at DHSS/DES/VCHC Joint Seminar on Early Intervention, Castle Priory, Wallingford, Berkshire.

O'Dell S. J., Tarler-Benlolo L. and Flynn J. M. (1979), An instrument to measure knowledge and behavioural principles as applied to children, *Journal of Behaviour Therapy and Experimental Psychiatry*, 10, 29-34.

Quine L. (1991), Sleep problems in children with severe mental handicap, *Journal of Mental Deficiency Research*, 35, 4, 269-290.

Quine L. and Pahl J. (1985), Examining the causes of stress in families with severely mentally handicapped children, *British Journal of Social Work*, 15, 501-517.

Quine L. and Wade K. (1991), *Sleep Problems in Children with Severe Learning Difficulties: An Investigation and an Intervention Trial*. Final Report to Rowntree Foundation, University of Kent at Canterbury.

Richman N., Douglas J., Hunt H., Lansdown R. and Levere R. (1985). Behahioural methods in the treatment of sleep disorders—a pilot study, *Journal of Child Psychology and Psychiatry*, 26, 581-590.

Rutter M., Tizard J. and Whitmore K. (1970), *Education, Health and Behaviour*, London, Longmans.

APPENDIX

Case Examples

Christopher

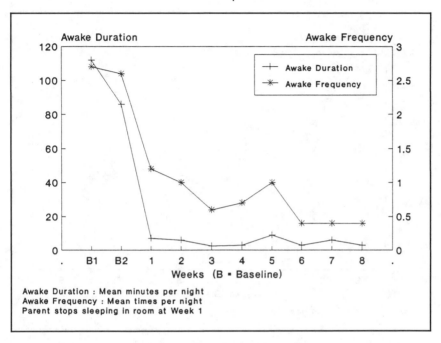

Awake Duration : Mean minutes per night
Awake Frequency : Mean times per night
Parent stops sleeping in room at Week 1

Christopher is an eleven-year-old boy with Down's Syndrome. He is continent and mobile. He can feed, wash and dress himself with help. He communicates by means of a mixture of speech and Makaton signs, and can understand simple language. He sometimes has periods of misery and irritability which can be difficult to deal with. He is sometimes aggressive and has a tendency to spit.

Christopher has had both a settling and a waking problem for as long as anyone can remember. He woke several times a night and came into his parents' room. One or other of his parents took him back to bed and usually ended up sleeping on a mattress near Christopher's bed. Treatment involved taking Christopher back to bed firmly and calmly whenever he got out of it, with a minimum of interaction, tucking him in and leaving him after a few minutes. His parents stopped sleeping on the floor of his room, from week one of treatment. Christopher was rewarded by being given a Disney sticker for his chart each time he did not disturb his parents at night.

Except for week 5, when he was ill, Christopher stopped coming into his parents room when he woke up, almost entirely, and his parents now no longer need to get up when he wakes. The total time he keeps his parents awake during the night has been reduced from over an hour and a half to about five minutes.

Jane

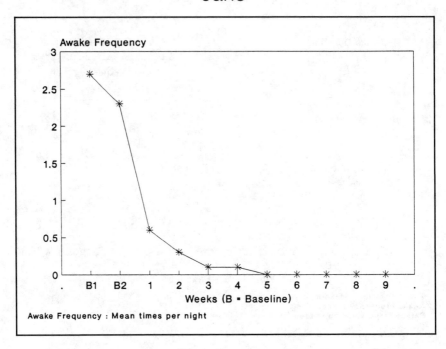

Awake Frequency : Mean times per night

Jane is a seven-year-old girl with moderate learning difficulties possibly due to microcephaly. She has some difficulty making herself understood by anyone other than close acquaintances. She is mobile and content during the day, but wets at night.

Jane shares a bedroom with her two sisters and this caused one of the problems; she talked to herself constantly and did not settle until around 10 p.m. The biggest problem for her parents, however, was waking during the night. When she wet the bed she screamed until the sheets were changed. This occurred 2 or 3 times a night, not necessarily due to wet sheets. If she was active during the day she slept through the night. The parents were only interested in tackling the waking problem although in the course of the programme they said they became much more consistent about bedtime. The aim of treatment was for Jane to lie quietly and not disturb her family when she woke during the night. The procedure was for Jane's mother to go to her when she woke up and tell her once and in a calm voice: "Go to sleep" unless she was wet. She was to sit a foot away and not approach the bed again. She was to ignore further requests to rearrange the bed clothes and to respond with a firm "No" if Jane screamed. The following morning Jane would be given lots of praise if she had behaved well during the night. She could also have a star for her chart if she didn't wet the bed.

The programme worked well. Jane's mother soon learned to stop giving Jane attention when she woke during the night. By the fifth week she was no longer disturbing her parents when she woke, and she has ceased to wet the bed.

Jenny

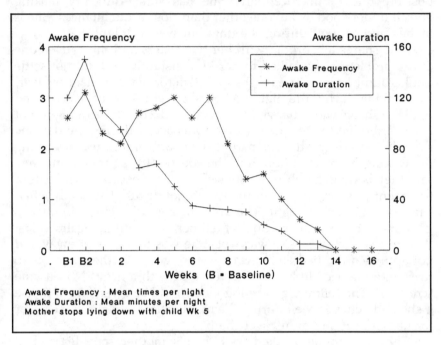

Awake Frequency : Mean times per night
Awake Duration : Mean minutes per night
Mother stops lying down with child Wk 5

Jenny is a three-and-a-half year old child with microcephaly and developmental delay. She is mobile but not yet continent. She has a 20-word vocabulary but can understand much of what is said to her. She has a number of behavioural problems. She is very dependent on her mother and continually seeks attention. She has frequent temper tantrums, is sometimes miserable and irritable and can be difficult to manage.

Jenny would not settle to sleep on her own. She insisted that her mother lay down on the bed with her, cuddling her closely as she fell asleep. She also woke two or three times a night and again her mother had to lie down with her until she returned to sleep. A graded approach to both settling and waking problems was used. Jenny's mother began by lying down with Jenny but not cuddling her. Jenny was given a teddy bear to cuddle instead. Jenny's mother gradually reduced contact with her daughter by lying down each night for a shorter time and moving to sit on a chair near the bed. By week 3 she was spending less time lying down with Jenny and more time sitting on the chair. When Jenny awoke during the night her mother sat by her bed until she fell asleep again. After a few weeks Jenny started coming into her parents' room when she woke. Jenny's mother took her straight back to bed, settled her and left the room.

By week 8 Jenny was able to settle to sleep alone in her own bed and her wakings were fewer. By week 11 she was scarcely waking at all. Jenny's mother is delighted with the results and is now expecting another child.

Jonathan

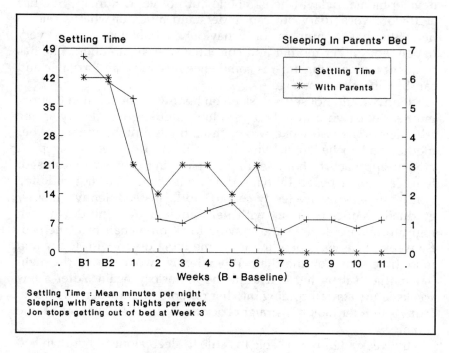

Settling Time : Mean minutes per night
Sleeping with Parents : Nights per week
Jon stops getting out of bed at Week 3

Jonathan is a five-year-old boy with severe learning difficulties of unknown cause. He is continent and able to walk. He can be quite difficult to manage, throwing temper tantrums, screaming and having periods of irritability and destructive behaviour. He communicates mainly by gesture or single words.

Jonathan had a severe settling problem and would spend a large part of each night in his parents' bed. Furthermore he would sleep for a couple of hours during the day and then not settle to sleep at night until very late, getting out of bed repeatedly and disturbing his parents with noisy behaviour. The aims of treatment were for Jonathan to cut out daytime naps and to remain in his bed and not call out at night. The procedure involved cutting down daytime naps gradually, allowing one hour for the first 3 days and then half an hour for the following 4 days and so on. At the same time a bedtime routine incorporating a story was introduced. If Jonathan was excited, his parents were to sit quietly by him and engage in no verbal or eye contact until he was calm and the story could begin. When Jonathan came into their room during the night, he was to be returned immediately to his own bed with minimal contact of any kind. Crying was to be ignored and appropriate behaviour was to be praised, immediately where possible, or the following morning. Jonathan's parents praised him immediately when he calmed down during settling time.

By the seventh week Jonathan had stopped getting into his parents' bed and his settling time was reduced from about an hour to about five minutes. Jonathan's parents felt that the bedtime story had a positively reinforcing effect on his settling behaviour.

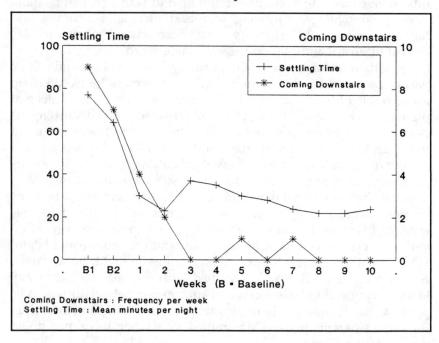

Mary

Coming Downstairs : Frequency per week
Settling Time : Mean minutes per night

Mary is a nine-year-old girl with Down's Syndrome. She is fully mobile and can understand communication related to her personal needs and make her own needs known. She has a number of daytime behavioural problems including aggression and attention-seeking.

Mary had severe settling problems, refusing to stay in her bed when she was settled for the night. Every night she either played about upstairs, shouting and throwing her toys around, disturbing her younger sister or she repeatedly came downstairs to her parents, refusing to go back to bed. She also woke two or three times during the night, disturbing her parents by calling for attention. Mary's mother said that she felt totally exhausted by the end of the evening.

Treatment involved deciding on a suitable bedtime for Mary and following a set routine every night. Mary was given a drink and biscuit and put to bed after a story and a cuddle. She was then put back to bed immediately every time she came downstairs or got up, with a minimum amount of interaction. The same course of action was followed when she awoke during the night. Mary was rewarded with praise if she stayed in bed. The treatment worked very rapidly, and Mary stopped waking at night completely. She also stopped getting out of bed except on a very few occasions when a verbal request was sufficient to get her back into bed. Settling time decreased from over an hour to about twenty minutes and Mary started to fall asleep about half an hour earlier. Mary's mother was delighted with the result and reported that Mary's daytime behaviour had also improved. She reported feeling less stressed, and better supported.

Stephen

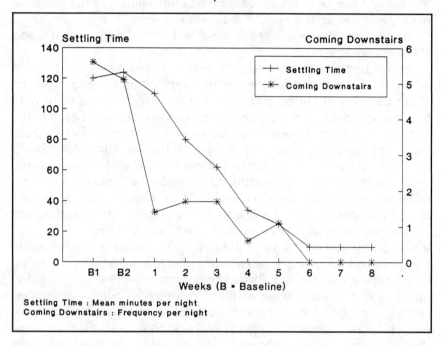

Settling Time : Mean minutes per night
Coming Downstairs : Frequency per night

Stephen is a twelve-and-a-half year old boy with moderate learning difficulties who had a bad hearing problem which was not detected until he was four. After seven operations over four years, his hearing has improved dramatically. He is mobile and continent and can feed, wash and dress himself without help. He is able to make himself understood by speech alone and can understand most of what is said to him. He is very difficult to manage, sometimes having periods of irritability or tantrums. He can be destructive and throw things about.

Stephen's severe settling problems dated from the time he was two-and-a-half years old and his sister was born. He was very demanding of attention in the evenings and would not go to sleep until his parents went up to bed. He would make a lot of noise in his room, disrupting his sister's sleep and come in and out of his room all evening, demanding food, drink, approval for his drawings, or anything that would force his parents' attention.

The aim of treatment was for Stephen to learn to be independent of his parents after a given time in the evenings and to be asleep by 10 o'clock. The programme required the parents to take Stephen upstairs to bed at 9 p.m., spend some quiet time reading with him or talking about his drawings and to settle him after a reminder of what was expected of him. If he appeared downstairs again, parents were not to allow themselves to be engaged in conversation or activity but to take him straight back up to bed. It was agreed that for every night Stephen remained upstairs, he would receive 20p towards a Ninja Turtle he wanted to buy. The treatment worked rapidly; by the sixth week, Stephen was no longer coming downstairs.

PART 3

Policy Development

CHAPTER 8

Developing Family Support in Local Authorities

Ruth Gardner

This chapter is derived from a National Children's Bureau development project, undertaken between 1987 and 1990 in two Social Services departments (Gardner, 1992). As the project was on a limited scale and the agencies were very different, we should be wary of generalising from the material presented here. However, many of the questions and issues that arose have been raised in other local authorities and voluntary agencies more recently, especially in connection with the Children Act.

I will give an overview of the two areas I worked in, what was done and the major points that emerge before linking these to possible developments for family support.

One of the study areas was in Surrey and included the county town and a population of about a quarter of a million, amidst 100 square miles of beautiful English countryside and some of the highest house prices in Britain. The area housing report mentioned 'severe housing disadvantage for certain sections of the community'—i.e. the elderly and young families unable to purchase their own homes. Nearly every manager and worker told me that the Council's first priority was to keep expenditure down, especially on Social Services.

The other area was in the London borough of Hammersmith and Fulham. This borough is just 11 square miles in its entirety, with a population of 152,000 including established Afro-Caribbean, Asian, Italian, Irish and Polish communities. Hammersmith and Fulham also had concern about its Social Service budget given a unique 1980s mix of community charge or poll-tax capping and losses on the stock exchange.

Given the huge difference in demography and demand in the two authorities, we did not set out to compare them directly but to describe preventive work as perceived by managers, social workers and parents and to see if any common themes emerged.

Forty workers in field work teams and family centres were questioned about their definition of family breakdown, their background, legal and policy knowledge, the kinds of tasks they undertook to prevent breakdown and tasks or activities they would have liked to undertake but were unable to, with the reasons. Less structured discussions took place with 15 senior and middle managers in social services, housing departments, units set up to promote good practice with Black and ethnic minorities and in a hospital.

Fifteen social workers, in both fieldwork teams and family centres were interviewed in detail about specific pieces of work in which they had preventive goals, and twelve of the parents involved in this work were also interviewed at length.

I undertook short pieces of work with the four teams. There were eight formal development sessions in all, as well as the three national seminars on prevention at the National Children's Bureau, bringing together examples of practice from around the country.

The development sessions with teams in Hammersmith and Surrey covered a wide range of practice issues which inform some of the ideas I put forward here. The social workers chose the topics and I researched them and came back with reading material and exercises which we used together for learning purposes (see Gardner, 1992).

One of the main achievements of the project, according to many of the workers, was that it interested them in looking afresh at what they did from a prevention perspective. Group supervisions with an outsider sometimes led to exploration of alternative answers to questions that the teams had been stuck with for some time. For instance they spent time mapping out the resources available on, or near, a particular estate rather than concentrating on individual referrals; or looking at health problems of parents as well as children with local health visitors, and finding ways to help families address these problems. Many workers said that they solely or habitually reviewed cases in terms of decisions to be taken *within a time frame*; this could close down options too quickly—whereas exploring overall preventive aims could relieve the immediate pressure and allow for some new ideas. This action of regularly reviewing and developing options seems to be fundamental in preventive work.

Four broad themes emerged from the very diverse written and interview material:

1. the frameworks for preventive social work (the law, policy, budgets);

2. local delivery of services, including referral processes etc.;

3. links with other preventive services;

4. preventive social work in practice—the perceptions of workers and parents.

In the full report we describe the services in place at the time, the settings in which they were provided and the infrastructure of policy and budgeting—then illustrate these from particular examples. The following summary picks out one or two of these.

Frameworks For Prevention

It may not surprise anyone that between a third and a half of interviewees (both workers and managers) did not know the current legal provisions (then the 1980 Act) for preventing the need for children to enter care or come before a court, for rehabilitation or for the facilitation of contact.

When asked about the law and prevention, most of those who knew of legislation mentioned duties concerning *prevention of harm* to children and a few mentioned Place of Safety Orders. This was despite the fact that workers defined family breakdown broadly; over half mentioned working to prevent deterioration of relationships, a quarter prevention of child abuse and a similar proportion prevention of reception into care (although statutory and voluntary care were rarely distinguished). Fewer than a quarter of allocated child care cases (children in care not included) involved children on At Risk registers. Although in most allocated cases there was some degree of concern about a child's welfare, this often arose because of angry scenes between adults or other stress in the household rather than deliberate or direct harm.

Preventing family breakdown thus appears to be a much wider activity than preventing significant harm to children, but the legal mandate for this wider activity was not apparently known to workers. It may not be necessary for social workers to know the letter of the law—although I would argue that increasingly they do need to understand the implications of different interpretations, and have up dates of test-cases, but it must surely be essential that they are well acquainted with agency policy on family support and its legal basis. They are otherwise in danger of acting unilaterally and disregarding users' rights, which could in turn make them the objects of official complaint.

The majority of workers and managers we interviewed were *not* aware of departmental policy on this subject. It took senior managers some time to discover the written statements, but the majority of people had not seen them at all, and only two team leaders out of the whole group had discussed prevention and family support in a management context. Hammersmith child care policy, which then relied heavily on permanency theory, did contain clear preventive goals, but set out in quite a complex way. Some form of introductory training is necessary to communicate policy, and the resources involved, effectively to workers.

Another problem seems to be, as the Surrey policy document stated, that "because prevention is a theme and not to be understood as a discrete service, the establishment of criteria is not necessary", a corollary of which is sometimes that "prevention as a theme of all social work does not appear to influence the distribution of resources... finance is not available specifically for promotion and support".

Diagram 1

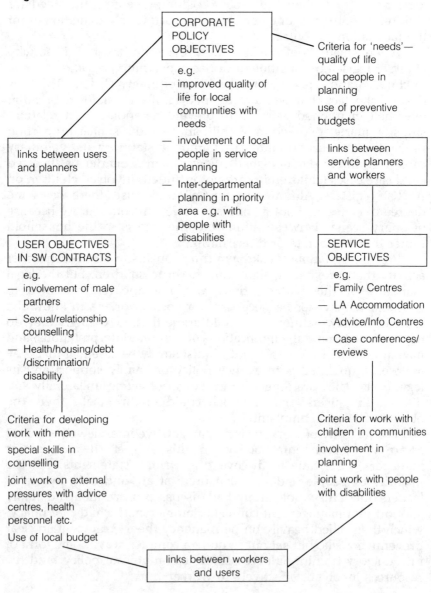

The Children Act 1989 begins to address this issue by setting out some of the discrete services that contribute to family support and by initiating a debate about standards and criteria with regard to day care and placement of children, for instance. Agencies also need much simpler and more accessible statements of their basic values and the ways in which these are underpinned by the law and policy. The services or activities which embody the policy should also be set out in writing, with their specific functions and objectives and how these relate to local needs. We later describe services which are flexible enough to respond to a variety of objectives, including the matters that family members themselves are requesting help with (*see diagram 1*).

Local Delivery of Services

There was a striking contrast (in both agencies) between the number and diversity of tasks undertaken with families, and the lack of any follow-up or evaluation of outcome in individual cases. Tasks or pieces of work often seemed to be ends in themselves, whereas for families on the verge of breakdown, planned work towards specific, agreed goals which could afterwards be reviewed was found helpful. Lack of re-referral was the most likely criterion of success being used, and even this was unreliable since referrals could not always be linked up. There was a dearth of hard information about the population served, the range of family problems, interventions and outcomes, the reasons for closing cases, discharging children from care or removing names from at risk registers.

Managers at local level argued a lack of administrative time to collect this information but it seemed there was also mistrust of its use at centre alongside measures of efficiency. They felt that efficiency was likely to be rewarded with more work, rather than rewards, such as time out for training.

Links with Other Services and Preventive Social Work in Practice
These two themes include a great diversity of work undertaken with families in these two agencies. Social workers were asked to detail some of the objectives of the preventive work they did. Objectives were often expressed in terms of tasks to be accomplished. These can be classified according to the *focus* of the activity (on the child, or the parents for instance), and according to the agency involved (social services, health etc.). Diagram 2 illustrates this classification.

Some matters of interest arise from this shopping list of preventive work. Firstly, workers in both agencies were undertaking a broadly similar range of tasks directed mostly at the child's development and the parental—in these cases that means largely the

Diagram 2
Social Workers Main Objectives in Preventive Work with Eight Surrey Families

	Examples
• **Child Focused** (8 responses)	— make sure the 3 year old gets to her playgroup; — try to enable the children to talk about possible sexual abuse.
• **Parent relationship with child** (7 responses)	— see if the mother can separate from the 2 year old more; — test parents' motivation to get child to the playgroup.
• **Adult relationship** (7 responses)	— sort out tasks and — give, or get expertise on, marital and sexual counselling.
• **Mother** (5 responses)	— mother to join a group for support.

Objectives involving other departments/agencies

• **Within social services** (8 responses)	— holiday play scheme to give mother a break; — get childminder and a playgroup to help with this child's development.
• **Health** (6 responses)	— respite care for a child with a mental handicap; — make sure the father's mental health is monitored by the GP and hospital.
• **Education** (4 responses)	— the child is bright but with behavioural problems—try to get special help without her removal from school.
• **Housing** (2 responses)	— about to be evicted for £400 rent arrears; — make representations to Housing.
• **Debt** (2 responses)	— try to obtain some expert debt counselling.

Social Workers Main Objectives in Preventive Work with Seven Families in Hammersmith & Fulham

	Examples
• **Child focused** (7 responses)	— monitoring of the children's play, development, health, responses to access; — more stimulation for the two youngest children; — enabling this teenager to be more independent while in touch with her parents, to improve her educational chances and be more confident in her racial and sexual identity; — checking the child was protected and safe;
• **Family relationships** including adult-adult and adult-child (6 responses)	— a full assessment of the possibility of rehabilitation, including the adult and parental relationships; — improve mother's ability to control the children without hurting them; — family meetings—so that the parents can negotiate who is to assume care of the child;

- **Mother focused**
  (5 responses)

  — temporary foster care and child-minding, for instance over hospitalisation;
  — practical help, for example with housing;
  — support and education for the mother in dealing with sexual abuse;

- **Child focused**
  (4 responses)

  — work with child must continue in case she wants to discuss sexual abuse in future;
  — more life story work with this teenager—the family history is so confusing;
  — continue to monitor any risk because of neglect of the childrens' emotional needs;

- **Adult relationship**
  (4 responses)

  — continuing efforts to bring the male cohabitee into work;
  — try to work on the grandmother's relationship with mother;
  — try to get mother to accept a psychiatric assessment.

- **Relationship with Child**
  (3 responses)

  — helping the mother and the child together on sexual abuse;
  — parents to try to co-operate in meeting the eldest boy's needs.

Objectives relating to other departments/agencies

- **Within Social Services**
  (14 responses)

  — we referred to The Family Centre for four-to-six weeks intensive work, a major part of our assessment.
  — we obtained a Day Nursery place, which is none too easy, for the three year old and the assistance of a family support worker to make sure he got there.
  — after the child came out of hospital he went straight to local foster carers on a Place of Safety. After that on a voluntary basis we worked towards rehabilitation. The foster carers were marvellous. Access ended up in the child's own home and the foster carers supported the natural parents all the way.
  — The Maya Project is for adolescent girls and she had her counsellor there for six months.

- **Health**
  (9 responses)

  — Health visitor alternating home visit and seeing parents at Health Centre, twice weekly, for monitoring purpose.
  — Great Ormond Street Hospital has been involved re possible sexual abuse.
  — The four year old has OP appointment re asthma.
  — Mother's mental health needed assessment which we were unable to do.

- **Education**
  (4 responses)

  — The school age children go to an after school play scheme run by ILEA.
  — There is an ILEA teacher at the Youth Project who has helped this teenager and her family.
  — The school were very worried by the eight year old's behaviour, and he will need long-term help.

- **Housing**
  (4 responses)

  — I obtained a single flat for the stepfather so as not to have to remove the children—a major preventive achievement, I thought.

  — I got her rehoused by the Borough away from her violent cohabitee.

  — She had to get here from Westminster where she was in B & B.

- **Other—Child Guidance**
  (2 responses)

  — Initially it was easier for the mother to go to Child Guidance about the sexual abuse, not as threatening as social services for her.

- **Refuge**
  (2 responses)

  — The Refuge gave her space, company and support, a play room, legal and practical advice and, after six months, the right to apply for permanent accommodation.

- **Solicitor**
  (1 response)

  — We helped her to get good legal advice about obtaining and maintaining an injunction.

- **Police**
  (1 response)

  — There is a good Domestic Violence Unit in the local police station. We work well with them and they have helped enforce the injunction so there is less damage to the house and disruption for the children.

maternal—relationships with the children. However, the Hammersmith workers more usually presented tasks as a programme of assessment or intervention, assessment often being the heading under which other agencies were brought in and involved in the process.

Secondly, workers relied on these other departments or agencies to undertake at **least half of the tasks** they wanted to accomplish. Their formal and informal leverage within and outside the departments was therefore of the essence, and if they lacked either sort of power or resources, the whole plan of work could drift and fall apart.

Finally, the blocks to progress which were felt by social workers and communicated to families seemed to be traceable to missing links between departments and agencies. In both authorities, the ad hoc nature of work with housing caused frustration; legal criteria, measures of need, priorities and procedures were different and there was no *formal* means of negotiating between them, although in Surrey a forum was set up between senior managers during the life of the project. Similarly debt and stress associated with financial problems were common issues for all the parents and yet work on this was often incidental or not completed, because specialist knowledge was not brought in or used in any planned way even where it was available.

Parents' Perceptions

So far as the parents interviewed were concerned, there were some important issues which were not given the same emphasis by workers. These included health and partnerships, including sexual relationships. It must be repeated here that the numbers were small, although similar points have emerged in other studies. Workers were aware of health problems as a stress factor but for parents they were of pressing concern, often both long-standing and serious. Among the twelve parents there had been depression and serious suicide attempts; gynaecological and pregnancy difficulties, eczema and psoriasis; cancer, alcoholism and heavy smoking. It was very rare to find work with health agencies in monitoring and improving *parental* health as opposed to children's, and yet it seems probable that this could have had a marked effect on parents' energy and capacity to enjoy their children, or indeed to undertake the tasks enjoined on them. This may explain the fact that while workers sometimes talked about the possibility of parents actively 'rejecting' or 'abandoning responsibility for' children, parents spoke in terms of having considered 'giving up' on the situation or of sheer despair and as we have said several had actually experienced degrees of mental or emotional breakdown.

The area of adult relationships in families raised a major difference in perception of family breakdown. Workers were firmly focussed on the **needs of children**—in particular the need for consistently good parenting. Most of the couples were not those that the children had been born to, and the mothers had provided most of the parenting consistency. The social work was almost exclusively undertaken by women with women and 'mothering skills' were the apparent criteria for judging parental success or failure.

'Family breakdown' was often summed up by workers in particular cases as "mother failing to meet children's needs or putting her own needs before the children's". For the women being worked with, the situation looked rather different. They were well aware of concerns about their mothering, but their most common definition of family breakdown, and much of their anxiety, centred on **loss of the adult relationship,** something they had usually experienced before.

Relationships with partners were often insecure and had negative aspects—arguments, sometimes abuse and sexual difficulties. Men had significant problems of their own which we mentioned earlier including histories of abuse, severe depression and alcoholism. Yet overwhelmingly women wanted to attempt to hang on to these relationships and the possibility of life as a family—understandably, given the poverty and low status of single parenthood.

Interviews with parents, some of whom were male partners, also indicated the positive side of the relationship—going out (however rarely) as a couple or a family, fathers sharing some of the child-rearing and some children responding positively to their male parent. Yet men were rarely seen or worked with by social services directly, and tended to be perceived as part of the problem rather than part of the solution. This may have been a correct perception in some instances but there was little evidence of its being tested out.

It seems that training, skills and resources are needed to give workers confidence to draw on the parental responsibility of fathers and father substitutes and to address their difficulties. Where men have acted threateningly, women workers need to feel safe doing this work. Family centres may be a particularly good venue and the resources to work family hours (i.e. evenings and weekends) rather than office hours would be essential. The family centres in the study had worked very successfully with couples, though this work was the exception. It was often difficult for the worker to address the sexual problems which seemed to underlie much of the distress in adult relationships. This required work by or with specialist counsellors and much joint discussion with the family to minimise confusion and secrecy.

Having mentioned some of the gaps, it is important to say that parents were highly appreciative of much of the work done. The provision of practical help such as day care and contributions in cash or kind, such as help with rent arrears, carpets, toys, Christmas presents for children were often mentioned. If workers 'stuck with' families through crisis, showed some understanding of the misery they were experiencing while remaining objective and honest, continued to be accessible for advice or support by phone if not by visits and looked for new ideas, parents said this reinforced their own efforts to keep going. Such work is likely to be consuming of workers' own energy and creativity and to demand special input and support.

Workers and parents did feel that 'breakdown' (however defined) had been averted. They had rarely had the opportunity given by the project to specify and to appreciate what they had achieved together, and plan future work based on their learning.

Developing Family Support Policy

As stated earlier, one major plank for developing family support work must be consistency of target-setting and evaluation, from overall policy objectives through to criteria and quality control for all services, to agreed work with individual families. Most important (especially in the context of organisational change) are the links, meaningful and lively forums for communication between interest groups at each of these levels, including councillors and senior managers; middle managers, professionals and volunteers; families, advocates and community groups of all kinds. Workers I spoke to asked for a clear mandate and legitimisation of preventive work, wanting their contact work with other agencies such as health centres, schools and voluntary agencies to be valued rather than seen as a luxury. They also might have been keener to ascertain families' views about outcome, and to report their own, had they had a stronger sense that managers valued successful preventive work in terms other than the saving of expenditure.

To summarise it appears that local authorities need much clearer and more succinct statements for workers and users alike, of their family support strategy and its legal basis. This should have a corporate basis with services provided by each department or section detailed. Budgets should allow for development work on support for particular needs. Workers and families found day care, family aides, local foster care, debt and relationship counselling and sensitive health advice among the most helpful resources and pilot studies of provision in these and other areas should monitor outcome with regard to particular services or packages. All family support services require regular monitoring and a senior manager or managers should have designated responsibility for overview and a regular public report.

Some examples of parts of the equation in place included efforts in both Surrey and Hammersmith to improve clients' access and status—in Surrey considerable resources had been used to make social services offices more local, attractive and welcoming as well as to develop a speedy complaints procedure, and Hammersmith had opened a brand new shop-front information service with a play area, which supplied free guidance on a wealth of welfare benefits, health, ethnic minority, women's and children's advice and support services, both statutory and voluntary. In Surrey, local control of budgets could allow for creative solutions to need without reference to the centre, while Hammersmith had protected certain preventive budgets, such as monies specifically for placements of children within the extended family. A combination of these central and local approaches might provide the greatest flexibility.

Taking in developments further afield, North Tyneside has successfully doubled its day care provision by generating income from a project called Childcare, which includes a range of services such as creches, advice to local businesses, nannies etc. This income has been used to protect and extend free day care for children in need. It is worth noting that the strategy is managed by a committee including senior officers from several departments as well as councillors, and that the plan is to take it out of exclusive social services control into a firmer interagency base. One of the strengths of this idea is again its shop-front operation, drawing on the wide popularity of the services to bring children in need and with disabilities into mainstream services.

The Children's Society's work with young people at Start Point in Torquay, together with East Devon Social Services, has provided a learning base for both agencies. Instead of responding directly to demand for residential accommodation, Start Point insisted on addressing some of the reasons for this demand, and as a result have developed a range of activities which offer much greater choice and flexibility of intervention and preclude the necessity of removing young people from home. They include a crisis intervention team for work with families, a support and information service, a leaving care support service and a remand supervision service, all backed by a small number of residential beds in two houses in the community.

Both these pieces of work have produced good information packs with statements of the philosophy and partnerships on which the work is based, the full range of services on offer and the types of need which they are intended to meet—with the clear intention of fitting provision as nearly as possible to individual families, rather than vice versa.

A City Council in the North has recently surveyed its housing provision for 16-17 year olds and come up with a number of findings which will require joint strategy on the part of housing and social services. Young people, whether care leavers or not, have tended to be slotted into inappropriate tenancies with little financial or other advice and support, thus leading to abandonment of the tenancy and vagrancy or unwanted relationships. The provision of a variety of supported housing, early interventions in debt and rent arrears, youth work rather than social work with young people and more focussed conciliation work between family members have emerged as preventive options.

Family Centres (in the broadest sense) as a 'hub' of services could include straight-forward community involvement in which the centre is used for local activities and 'owned' by its neighbourhood; early identification of possible needs and low-level responses such as recreational and social opportunities for whole families; and focussed work with particular difficulties. This would not necessarily all take place in the one venue but in various forms of outreach work and in a number of settings.

Family centres could carry that most important duty, to enable families to receive support before their children's health and development is in jeopardy. Given the range of skills already available in many family centres, which can include teaching, health, care training, youth and community development work, this seems very appropriate. Family centres are in some agencies being located as the main 'providers' of child care work of all kinds; adequate resourcing will be vital if they are to take on more of field workers' statutory functions as well as their current preventive activities. Otherwise important family support skills will be lost.

Diagram 3
Family Support

A. Clear mandate: Values, Law, Corporate policy, Financing Implications include:
- clear communication of mandate/policy via statements and induction training;
- specific budgets including development funds with some local controls;
- specific staffing resources.

B. Capacity to re-assess need at child/family/neighbourhood level, consistently reviewing options with families.
Implications include:
- skills in open assessment/negotiation/challenging local systems and decisions;
- inclusion of vol/community work in family support;
- encouraging advocacy on behalf of families by independent persons/agencies.

C. Linked preventive options from informal, low-key to intensive, with a range of settings and skills.
Implications include:
- joint funding between departments and sectors with medium/long term family support programmes;
- re-use of settings e.g. advice centre for residential home;
- dialogues re options between potential users, purchasers and providers.

D. Regular evaluation of outcome against specific criteria e.g.
What does each party to family support want to get out of it? What would a good service provide towards meeting their needs?
Implications include:
- rewards for good practice;
- actually talking to children and adults;
- acceptance of purpose of evaluation i.e. regular explicit feedback into policy.

The idea of clusters of services geared to central family support activity which includes the monitoring of decision-making and outcomes and in some cases the budgeting and purchasing functions, thus begins to emerge clearly in a number of different contexts. It allows for linkage between low-key advice, intensive support and particular resources such as housing, family aides or day care (diagram 3). It must be capable of drawing on local people's *own* definitions of need and the ways in which they would like to see them met, on statutory and voluntary provisions.

It is important not to lose the opportunity of tracing new developments under the Children Act 1989 and, most significantly, how they are perceived by and affect families over both the short and the longer term. This is where resources now have to be found, assisting social workers and others to undertake the evaluation and follow-up which has been largely missing to date.

References

Gardner, R. (1992) *Supporting Families: Preventive Social Work in Practice.* London: National Children's Bureau.

CHAPTER 9

Local Authority Policies on Children in Need

Jane Tunstill

Introduction

The 1989 Children Act introduces a new legislative framework for
family support work, based on a duty to provide services for
'children in need and their families'. This chapter provides a brief
policy background to the changes; points to some specific challenges
for local authorities in implementing them; identifies existing as well
as proposed monitoring mechanisms; and concludes with some
suggested components of an implementation strategy.

The extent and nature of the work carried out with parents to
enable a child to stay at home rather than become the voluntary or
involuntary recipient of state substitute care has exercised the minds
of policy makers, both descriptively and prescriptively, for at least
the last five decades. The relevant literature in the same period
contains two apparently incompatible themes. On the one hand
there is widespread acknowledgement of the centrality of the issue:

> "While there is a general acceptance that more could and should be
> done explicitly to prevent children entering long term care, and some
> awareness of the courses of action that would make this possible, there
> is as yet regrettably little indication of any concerted strategy which
> could translate pious thought into action..." (House of Commons,
> 1984, para. 30).

On the other hand successive studies question the extent to which
effective family support is ever a policy and practice priority; Farmer
and Parker are only the latest in a line of researchers to pose such
a question.

> "Saddest of all would be our failure to prevent children being
> committed to care who did not need to be subject to such drastic
> intervention. Our study must at least place something of a question
> mark over that issue given the relatively high rate of 'successful'
> placements back home that the results revealed" (Farmer and Parker,
> 1992, page 191).

The 1989 Children Act adds a new dimension to this discrepancy between ideal and practice by expanding considerably the duties and powers of local authorities in respect of family support but simultaneously defining a category of children at whom those duties and powers are directed. Doubt has been expressed as to whether imposing this new requirement to 'target' resources will necessarily lead to improvements in service delivery and outcome for parents and their children. There is arguably now an additional imperative for 'getting it right' because the 1989 act establishes a new balance between the protection of children and the rights of parents. "In many respects the success or failure of the Children Act 1989 will depend upon the extent to which the Part III provisions are implemented" (Williams, 1992, page 15).

In Need: Policy Perspective on a New Concept
There are several characteristics which distinguish the family support functions in this act from earlier legislation. They include the relatively broader definition of local authorities' powers to assist families; the freeing of such powers from a simple connection with prevention of reception into care or remaining in care; and perhaps more importantly, the new emphasis on providing services to 'children in need and their families' rather than to an un-differentiated potential population who might at some stage run the risk of reception into care. In the course of the passage of the Children Bill through parliament it was this aspect—an apparent narrowing of access to (paradoxically wider) services—which united voluntary organisations against it, and led to two failed amendments seeking respectively to remove the notion of 'in need' or to add the wording 'likely to be in need'. It was perceived at that early stage by the organisations as a problematic concept, and concerns have continued to be expressed (Tunstill, 1991).

Attention has focused in particular on the way in which local authorities are constructing a relationship between Sections 17(1) and 17(10).

17(1)   'It shall be the general duty of every local authority...
(a) to safeguard and promote the welfare of children within their area who are in need; and
(b) so far as is consistent with that duty, to promote the upbringing of such children by their families, by promoting a range and level of services appropriate to those childrens' needs'.

and

17(10)   For the purposes of this Part a child shall be taken to be in need
if—
(a) he is unlikely to achieve or maintain, or to have the
opportunity of achieving or maintaining a reasonable standard
of health or development without the provision for him of such
services

or

(b) his health or development is likely to be significantly
impaired, or further impaired, without the provision for him of
such services

or

(c) he is disabled.

It is only possible to begin to understand the characteristics of policy
development within local authorities around Section 17 by taking as
much account of the Guidance and Regulations as of the clauses on
the face of the act. In many ways Volume II provides a case study
of the tensions between **discretion** and **mandate** which have always
bedevilled the 'preventive' child care work of the state.

"This guidance does not lay down firm criteria or set general priorities
because the Act requires each authority to decide their own level and
scale of services appropriates to the children in need in their area..."
Para.(2.4). And further on: "local authorities are not expected to meet
every individual need, but they are asked to identify the extent of need
and then make decisions on the priorities for service provision in their
area in the context of that information and their statutory duties".
(Department of Health, 1991, para. 2.11).

The volume deals relatively briefly with the definition of In Need,
Assessment, Planning and the Meeting of Need and in fact lays
down few specific requirements. While Part III and Schedule 2
"provides a clear remit to local authorities for the provision of
services to children in need and their families" (Gibbons, 1991), the
Guidance, by its emphasis on local discretion and the necessity for
prioritisation, calls attention to the discretionary elements of the Act
itself. The Act, as well as the Guidance, give room to discretion in
the policies of local authorities as well as in the practice of indvidual
social workers.

At the time of writing it is far too early to have a clear picture of
how the Act is being implemented in general, let alone any
substantial data about Section 17. There were however signs as long
ago as 1990 that in the context of considerable financial stringency in
public spending, some local authorities were approaching this
particular implementation task in a 'minimalist' way, and in some
cases replacing the definition of 'in need' in the act with more

restrictive definitions of their own, which limited their provision of services to children at clear risk of significant harm. These developments prompted the Department of Health to write to all Directors of Social Services at the beginning of 1991, making it clear that such strategies were unacceptable. (This proscription was subsequently incorporated in the Guidance and Regulations, Volume II, para. 2.4).

Certainly confusion has been evident amongst both social workers and the professional groups with whom they are likely to be closely involved, including health professionals. A survey carried out by the Health Visitors Association in September 1991 revealed that health visitors themselves had little clear understanding of the definition of 'in need'; 283 health visitors in 99 health authorities in England and Wales were asked to estimate the number of children under 5 on their caseloads who could be defined as 'in need' under the Act's provisions; 23 per cent claimed none; and 45 per cent said between one and ten only, in caseloads averaging just over 300. A more realistic assessment, suggested by the Health Visitors Association, would be at least 90 children (30 per cent) in a relatively affluent caseload, and up to 270 (90 per cent) in an area of high deprivation (Health Visitors Association, 1991).

Particular Challenges for Local Authorities in Implementing Section 17

It is some time since child care commentators, policy makers or practitioners gave up the illusion that their arguments existed in a neutral ideological vacuum:

> "Child care and the role of society acting through the state are rightly seen as of crucial importance to society, but the issues are complex and tied to deep-seated values and feelings... there is no certainty and no consensus as to the state's role in child care..." (Fox Harding, 1991).

This complexity applies to the choice of factors to be taken account of in any decision as well as to the nature of the decision itself and so there is no **absolute** agreement about which factors pose the greatest challenges to the design of policy on Section 17. It is difficult however to ignore the following issues.

(a) Children in need are likely to come from fairly distinct socio-economic groups

There is a strong association between poverty and material deprivation and reception into care. This has been a theme in child care research for some time, and was underlined by the conclusion of the Short Committee that 'children in care are the children of the poor'; research continues to support the same message.

Bebbington and Miles (1989) examined the data on the characteristics of children in care and arrived at an estimation of the relative chances of children from different backgrounds being received into care. 'Child A' living in a white, two parent family, with no dependence on social security, two or fewer children in the family, and an owner-occupied house with more rooms than people, has a one in seven thousand chance of being received into care. 'Child B' on the other hand, in a single adult household of mixed ethnic origin, with the household head drawing income support, four or more children in the family, and a privately rented home with more people than rooms has a one in ten chance of being received into care. Rowe's study (1989) of over 2,000 placement decisions 'reinforced the message that children in need were not charateristically children whose parents were abusive or neglectful. It showed a preponderance of admissions due to material crises (homelessness, debt) or behavioural problems, with parents motivated by their children's welfare. . .' Bradshaw (1990) has revealed the dramatic increase in the numbers of children in the population living in poverty, a doubling in fact in the last decade.

Such data reveal the scale of material deprivation. Social Security, not local authority social services, has prime responsibility for income maintanance. Nevertheless, the Act's definition of children in need does embrace problems likely to be caused by material deprivation. There may be implications for the way in which social services departments organise and deliver their own services as well as seek to obtain the offer of services from other departments in a corporate approach to need. While the notion of an anti-poverty strategy, as such, is often seen as politically sensitive, there may be considerable implications for family income levels within Section 17, in particular the day care clauses, which could usefully be explored. What the research does underline is the necessity of taking account of the material circumstances of childrens' lives in both the organisation of services and the nature of the assessment system.

(b) The Continuum between Prevention and Protection

In the debates about the ideal ends and means of child care policy it has often seemed that 'prevention' and 'protection' have been artificially polarised. Respective adherents of the 'state paternalism/child protection' and the 'defence of the birth family/parents' rights' schools of thought (see Fox Harding, 1991) may have appeared to espouse very different explanations and answers. This has meant that those in the latter category have failed to highlight the essentially 'protective' implications of the provisions they supported, while those in the former paid too little attention to the need to offer non-stigmatising, accessible and attractive family support services. As Packman and Jordan point out, the research studies of the 1980s.

> "recognised a kind of mismatch between the very different elements in the work of services for families and children, and the unhelpfulness of the legalistic and adversarial approach to most of the work... legalism and the exclusion of parents would have paradoxical consequences: the last resort philosophy and pessimism about care could lead to reluctance to recognise the signs of abuse, which in turn especially in a hard-pressed and under-resourced situation. . . could have fatal results" (Packman and Jordan, 1991).

The 1989 Act is concerned to get away from the hazards of earlier approaches, but this puts a very heavy responsibility on local authorities to set up their family support systems in a way which does not deter parents from asking for help early on, and which will not contain an 'inflationary' element, so that a request for help will be rewritten as an acknowledgement of abuse or neglect. Section 17 (10) of the Act provides an all-embracing definition of children in need which should prevent a limiting focus on one aspect of need. Local authorities, therefore, should not be tempted into restricting access to their family support services to children who are seen to be at considerable risk of abuse. Such a policy would stigmatise the family support services on offer and quite probably deter many parents from approaching them for help. Such an outcome would be a reversal of the intentions of the act.

(c) The Need to Ensure Harmony with the Principles which Underpin the Act
One of the novel characteristics of the 1989 act is the extent to which it was preceded by an explicit debate about values, and the publication by the Department of Health of *Principles and Practice in Guidance and Regulations* (Department of Health, 1989).

There are a number of principles of relevance to family support, including;

• partnership with parents

• the importance of families

• the importance of the views of the child.

Existing and Proposed Monitoring

It will be some time before we can begin to reach clear conclusions about the extent to which the Children Act may change the culture of social service departments, as its architects intended. Monitoring of Section 17 has been regarded as especially difficult, and the first administration of the revised forms for local authority statistical returns to the Department of Health in 1992 will exclude questions about 'children in need'. One of the factors in this delay must be the difficulties posed by the diversity in approaches arising from the cumulative discretion inherent in both the clauses of the act and the guidance. The statistical returns **will** include questions about Section 17 from 1993, and it is likely that Department of Health commissioned research will by then have produced information about the way in which local authorities are designing and implementing their policies. (Aldgate and Tunstill, 1992).

Some general trends are already discernible from the policy statements which local authorities have so far produced; these have been examined and tentatively analysed in different quarters.

The 'In Need Implementation Group' (NCVCCO, 1991), set up by organisations in the voluntary sector in 1990 (with both statutory and voluntary members) to express concerns about the apparent trends evident then, studied forty such policy statements. It concluded that the dominant approach was to produce a list of those children who would have priority access to Section 17 services, and that there was a tendency to use the notion of 'primary, secondary and tertiary level intervention' developed by Hardiker et al (1991) to categorise the needs of the children and their families. Where local authorities used this approach they commonly categorised children in the 'tertiary' category as in this example from a London borough:

> "Children who are on the child protection register for sexual, physical or emotional abuse or neglect and are the subject of a Court order. Children who are not on the child protection register but are the subject of a Court order, which specifies or directs involvement from the local authority. i.e. care order, child assessment order, emergency protection order, supervision order, criminal supervision order (with or without a residence requirement). Children or young people remanded to or detained in local authority accommodation. Young people detained or at risk of detention in secure accommodation or custody".

In many of the authorities adopting such an approach there was a clear statement that priority would be likely to be accorded to the children in this tertiary group. However, such findings must be seen as tentative given the 'transient' nature of many of the documents studied; some will have been draft statements of policy, others the final version (at least until altered at a later stage).

Similarly the National Council for Voluntary Child Care Organisations examined the policy statements of fourteen Midland authorities. In interpreting the Act's definition of 'In Need' thirteen of the fourteen used a 'priority list' approach, eleven based on an (albeit subjective) "broad" definition of need, two on a (comparably subjective) "narrow" definition. Three of the sample stressed the universal/non-stigmatising nature of their services, and seven the importance of participation by parents. As regards a corporate approach, this was only evident in nine of the documents, and the contribution of the voluntary sector figured in only five of them (NCVCCO, 1992).

Clearly what is required is a coherent and consistent approach to monitoring, even given the complexities of research in this area. It is likely that the monitoring exercise undertaken in April/May 1992 by London region Social Services Inspectorate (1992) was the first attempt to look at the implementation of the act as a whole. Instead of inferring approaches from published documents, this study was based on a questionnaire administered to all thirty three London boroughs, with a response from twenty nine of them. Methodology also included the eliciting of qualitative material in a series of face to face interviews with local authority and voluntary sector managers.

London authorities varied as to how they had gone about identifying and assessing children in need. The majority had done this through meetings with other statutory agencies (23), meetings between departments in the authority (25) and to a lesser extent circulation of documents to other agencies (17) and meetings with voluntary organisations (13). Only three boroughs had held public consultation meetings, which perhaps indicates rather disappointingly a missed opportunity to involve parents themselves in the dabate about policies.

There were also indications of either existing or future tensions between the various departments in a local authority. Asked to indicate which agencies in the area accepted a common system of priorities for 'need' as entitling access to their services, there was a far from united approach on the part of social services, education,housing and in addition health authorities. Fourteen education departments, thirteen housing departments, seven district health authorities and five family health services authorities shared the common system of priorities. For leisure departments, probation and voluntary agencies the figures were respectively nine, two and three. Without a more ambitious study it would be difficult to understand all the reasons, but differences in ideology seem certain to play a part. Education departments, for example, see themselves as providing a universal service, and are reluctant to restrict their service delivery to selective categories. In fact in one of the boroughs studied the heads of the day nurseries had been specifically instructed **not** to allocate all their places to 'children in need' but to strive to maintain a balanced population.

The questionnaire design took as read the strategy of prioritising need, and asked the boroughs to indicate which groups of children they regarded as high priority in assessing individual need. Some groups commanded a priority rating in every local authority, namely children at risk of abuse or neglect, children in care and children with disabilities. Others came a narrow second; children accommodated under Section 20(27); children placed out of borough (26); young people on remand (23). A 'middle band' included young people on remand and in the penal system (17); children with special educational needs (15); carers with mental illness (15); children under 8 (14); black and ethnic minority families (14); families in Bed and Breakfast (13). There was however a group who failed to secure a high rating, including, perhaps most worryingly given the socio-economic data mentioned above, families on income support and family credit (4), one parent families (5) and unemployed parents (8), although families whose gas and electricity had been disconnected were chosen as a high priority by eleven.

Final conclusions must await more extensive investigation but it may appear so far that most local authorities are taking a rather less proactive approach than the architects of the act may have hoped, and that the effect of the new provision to assess children as 'in need' is to narrow and stigmatise provision. As some of the managers interviewed in the London exercise said, the entitlement to family support services under this act is narrower than under the previous legislation.

Towards an Implementation Strategy for Section 17

However, there is still a debate to be had about the way in which the family support clauses might be implemented to provide a firm foundation for policy. The following eight strategic objectives were selected by the In Need Implementation Group (1991) and have subsequently been adopted by several social services departments. They are all derived entirely from the requirements of the act, and they are by no means all resource intensive.

(1) Services for all children

It should be recognised that all children have needs, albeit different ones, and services should be provided without stigmatising or pathologising the recipients. It is logical therefore to provide a range of services, which at one end might meet complex needs, and at the other very simple ones... Complex assessment will not always be necessary (an economy in itself), and some services might be provided by open access. 'Universalism' should inform the whole style and structure of policy formulation and service delivery.

(2) Creativity
The 1989 Act is based on new ways of thinking about child care which have their roots in research. It is intended to challenge some of the unhelpful 'dogma' of the past, and creative policy might need to involve asking questions about the sanctity of existing budgets, and perhaps moving resources from other parts of the child care budget or for that matter from other departments to use in family support. A truly corporate response might see some services being provided under Part 3 without service users ever setting foot in a social services department. This objective would fit closely with those concerning universalism and partnership.

(3) Commitment to assess need
It is important that need is assessed and information aggregated. If local authorities only keep information on met need, and fail to record the extent of unmet need, demand will inevitably be suppressed. It is crucial that they record the unmet need, and its resource implications, and pass the data on to councillors, M.P.s and central government as well as using them within their own development plans.

(4) The promotion of mixed economy of service provision
Section 17 requires local authorities to involve the voluntary sector in service delivery, and there are many exciting opportunities to develop strategic partnerships with voluntary organisations at local and national level. Research demonstrates the way in which service users appreciate 'choice' (Holman, 1988) and in addition it is often the case that voluntary organisations are most responsive to the ethnic or cultural dimensions of local need.

(5) The provision of a range and breadth of services
The most appropriate way of providing services is along a continuum. It is also important for services to be perceived as directly relevant to a community or locality, for example being provided in a particular language, thus bringing life to those parts of the act dealing with race, language and culture.

(6) The commitment to publicise services
The act requires local authorities to publicise services, and this should be seen as a way of empowering service users. It needs to

take account of ethnic composition, and above all information policies should be based on the question "If I were a stranger here, how long would it take me to find out what is on offer for my child's needs?".

(7) **Partnership**

The concept of partnership should underpin relationships between the local authority and parents; the wider family; neighbours and net-works in the community; voluntary organisations; private organisations; with other local authority departments; and with other statutory agencies.

(8) **Accountability**

There has to be a high priority for monitoring, evaluating and promoting service quality. Complaints and representations procedures are one key component, and should be used as a way of testing the responsiveness of a service as well as dealing with formal complaints. If used in this way they signal a concern on the part of the local authority about the adequacy of their response to the individuals and communities they serve.

Conclusion

Policy development within Part Three of the act represents the linchpin for an appropriate child care system in every local authority. The broad intentions of the Act, and the broad definition of need in Section 17, must not be distorted by a minimalist reading of the Guidance and Regulations. It is important for local authorities to select the right strategic objectives to avoid the pitfalls and eight have been suggested.

References

Aldgate, J. and Tunstill, J. (1992). Oxford University: Unpublished.

Bebbington, A. and Miles, J. (1989). The background of children who enter local authority care. *British Journal of Social Work*, 19, 5, 349-368.

Bradshaw, J. (1990). *Child Poverty and Deprivation in the UK*. London: National Childrens Bureau.

Department of Health (1989). *The Care of Children: Principles and Practice in Regulations and Guidance*. London: HMSO.

Department of Health (1991). *The Children Act 1989, Guidance and Regulations, Volume 2, Family Support, Day Care and Educational Provision for Young Children.* London: HMSO.

Farmer, D. and Parker, R. *Trials and Tribulations.* London: HMSO.

Fox Harding, L. (1991). *Perspectives in Child Care Policy.* London: Longman.

Gibbons, J. (1991). Children in need and their families: outcomes of referral to social services. *British Journal of Social Work,* 21, 217-227.

Hardiker, P., Exton, K. & Barker, M. (1991). *Policies and Practices in Preventive Child Care.* Aldershot: Gower.

Health Visitors Association (1991). *The Children Act and Health Visitors.* London: Health Visitors Association.

Holman, B. (1988). *Putting Families First; Prevention and Child Care.* London: Macmillan.

House of Commons (1984). *Second report from the Social Services Committee. Session 1983-84, Children in Care.* London: HMSO.

In Need Implementation Group (1991). *The Children Act and Children's Needs; Make It the Answer Not the Problem.* NCVCCO.

National Council for Voluntary Child Care Organisations (1992). *Midlands Local Authorities Definition of Children In Need.* London: NCVCCO.

Packman, J. and Jordan, B. (1991). The Children Act: looking forward, looking back. *British Journal of Social Work,* 21, 315-327.

Rowe, J., Hundleby, M. and Garnett, L., *Child Care Now,* BAAF 1989, quoted in Packman, J. and Jordan, B. (1991). *op. cit.*

Social Services Inspectorate London Region (1992). *Capitalising on The Act.* London: SSI.

Tunstill, J. (1991). 'The Children Act and the voluntary childcare sector'. *Children and Society* 5.1.

Williams, J. (1992). *The Children Act 1989: The public Law.* London: HMSO.

CHAPTER 10
SUMMING UP
The Research Aspects

Roy Parker

Knowledge about Family Support

In considering these studies one is made aware of how much more we do know now than we did before about family support—about its organisation, the groups involved and some of the implications of its provision. Some of these gains in knowledge may seem slight, but when one compares them with the situation even five years ago they assume considerable importance. Of course, the more studies there are, the more bricks with which we have to build; but it is a slow process. Simply because we know more does not mean that we know immediately what better to do. There are various steps in between and we are probably still at a fairly early stage in the process. Nevertheless, let us consider some of the matters that have been highlighted by the researches. At least half a dozen areas stood out for me.

First there was the extent to which the schemes described had been successful in identifying and reaching families in need. The groups who used these support services were incontestably in need, by whatever criteria one chooses to apply.

The second thing that struck me, (as it has over the years in a whole range of child and family care research), was the considerable extent of ill-health that existed, both amongst the adults and the children. The whole health dimension of 'need' cries out to be more closely integrated with policies and practices aimed at family support. There is a similar need to include questions of housing. For example, many parents in the studies seemed to lack safe, controllable and stimulating space for their children. Good housing is not only a matter of adequate and affordable living space inside, especially where children are concerned.

Thirdly, the prevalence of lone parenthood amongst the groups using the family support services was considerable. But both the reality and the concept of lone parenthood need to be disaggregated so that we understand better what it actually means to those involved. There is still a tendency to regard the whole range of lone parents as a common category simply because, at any one time, they are without a partner. That is not to deny that lone parenthood can be an important factor in creating the need for support, but its variations must be taken into account; for example, in terms of when it occurs, its duration and what it has superseded.

Fourthly, I was impresssed by what parents reported about their needs and problems, especially their appeals for respite. Many seemed to be isolated, but isolated with children. They sought some form of relief from the continuing interaction with children and from the wear and tear that that entailed.

A fifth aspect of the studies seemed to be the high rate of geographical mobility amongst the families. This raises important questions about the kinds and levels of informal support that highly mobile families can call upon as well as other issues about what provokes such frequent mobility and what that in its turn implies for the organisation of family support services. After all, if we insist on providing services in fixed locations, people who move from place to place a lot are unlikely to get much sustained help.

Finally, there are the ever-present and dominating problems of income and associated with that, of debt. However, I noted that the studies did not consider income per head although we know from a range of poverty studies that it is not only low wages or having to live on benefits that plunge families into deep poverty but also the number of people amongst whom a particular income has to be shared.

Conceptual Frameworks

With these studies we have moved forward in creating a set of ideas and frameworks, largely through the process of classification. This is of the utmost importance because empirical research, conceptualisation and theorising have to go together hand-in-hand if we are to advance our understanding and thereby improve practice.

For instance, these studies provided new ideas about the classification of families' needs, the nature of support in terms of its quality, quantity and timing, as well as whether it is instrumental or emotional. Moreover, we now have some basis for conceptualising the nature of the services which might form an effective system of family support. There were also some very interesting yet basically simple ideas for the classification of the dimensions of parenting; for exmple, anticipation, autonomy, co-operation, control and so on.

Lastly, there were some important suggestions about the way research in this field may be developed. In particular I was impressed by the extent to which many of the studies had been able to tap what consumers said and what they thought. There also seemed to be exciting possibilities for the use of close observation and video-taping, not just as a research tool but also as a means by which research results could be fed back quickly—both into practice and to the families who collaborated with the researchers. Too often research goes on for several years, with the feedback often taking even longer and then being made available primarily to managers and policy-makers rather than to practitioners and participants. The studies reported here provided some refreshing ideas about how research results can be presented (for example by means of videos) so that they have a better chance of being absorbed into both professional and parenting practice.

Outstanding Questions

Inevitably, the studies leave many questions outstanding. There were indeed some interesting assumptions and omissions. One of the assumptions seemed to be that family support was needed primarily by families with young children. However, if one takes the provision of 'accommodation' or admission to care as crude indices of points of risk, then as well as the high 'risk' for children under one, there is also a high risk again at about twelve to fourteen. One has to consider therefore the extent to which these studies are generalisable to families with older children, or to families with a range of children of different ages—and of course with the formation of step-families, second marriages and new cohabitations, the likelihood of there being children of mixed ages becomes greater.

Furthermore, if we are attempting to devise support services for families how should we approach the question of their duration? Different answers have profoundly different implications for the distribution of resources and for the development of policy more generally. For example, the study that Elaine Farmer and I recently completed on children home on trial (Farmer & Parker, 1990) certainly raised that question. There was a minority of families where the children went home under very adverse conditions but a tolerable state of affairs was achieved by an enormous and continuing social work input of resources. One has to ask what would happen in such circumstances were these removed or reduced. The question then arises of how scarce resources are distributed as between those families where a 'free-standing' improvement can be made in the relatively short-term and those where support may well have to be provided for long years.

In relation to disability, one wonders how far some of the conclusions of the studies were equally applicable to families with disabled children. Not all such families will be in the extreme situations that some of the projects describe, but they may need a good deal of support and help. That, more generally, raises the question of families on the margin of need. How far does the concentration of services on priority groups worsen the position of 'intermediate' groups; for example groups with apparently less pressing needs but needs which may accumulate or steadily wear down families over the years.

Not much was said about how far the ideas and results obtained by the research could be generalised to different ethnic groups. For example, we are currently undertaking further analyses of the massive OPCS disability survey, part of which was a major enquiry into disabled children in the community and in residential care (Meltzer et al., 1989). From our work on the 'communal establishments' survey we are finding differences in the levels and types of disability amongst children of different ethnic backgrounds. This (and there are other examples) sounds a cautionary note about the dangers of assuming that there are basically similar needs across a whole range of groups, whether they be determined by class, age or ethnicity.

May I conclude with a point that Richard Titmuss made many years ago? He argued that one could not understand the full impact of welfare provisions unless one also understood the mechanisms that were operating to create *dis-welfares*. In endeavouring to design and supply 'support' it is incumbent upon us to try to understand the social mechanisms that operate to create what might be called *dis-support*. In this respect one of the important omissions in several of the studies may well have been a consideration of the role of men—the way that their behaviour creates *dis-supports* in families and around children.

References

Farmer, D. and Parker, R. (1990). *Trials and Tribulations*. London: HMSO.

Meltzer, H., Smyth, M. and Robus, N. (1989). *Disabled Children: Services, Transport and Education: OPCS Surveys of Disability in Great Britain, Report 6*. London: HMSO.

CHAPTER 11

A Director's Perspective

Ian White

I shall contribute a director's eye view of the world, which is not necessarily the same view of the world as the one informing earlier chapters, because, in my job, I'm interested not only in the learning but also in the implementation. There are light years of difference between the two and many of the problems (as in any organisation) are to do with converting learning into systematic, basic, day-to-day, ongoing practice.

Stage of Implementation of the Children Act
I must repeat the warning that in my view it is entirely wrong to make a judgement about the quality of the implementation of the Act just a month after it came into force. We in Oxfordshire have set ourselves short-term goals for the last twelve months: to get the basic systems in place, the basic front line staff trained and the basic knowledge as far as we can embedded in the organisation. That, in itself a huge undertaking, is phase one which isn't yet over. So in thinking about family support we need to see it alongside all the other aspects of the Children Act and children's services, not least residential childcare.

One has to see the development of thinking about family support over a longer period than just a month or even a year, and I would expect that good departments would be doing certain things now as part of defining a children's strategy. I would expect them to try and map out where residential care fits with other forms of care, which fit with family support, which in turn fits with various other things. I would expect them to be defining operational briefs for different parts of that pattern of services, and some of the studies represented in this book, if they are disseminated well, will be important contributions to this process. It is very important that as research comes off the production line it is converted into a different format for the different people who are going to use it. It needs to be converted into operational briefs, practice checklists and so on.

Most authorities are going through a period of re-focussing at the moment. I would counsel people not to take anything for granted and not to make broad assumptions that are not applicable, not to forget what is already happening in the field—the burgeoning sponsored child-minding schemes, the family centres that already exist, the contracts that exist between local authorities and voluntary organisations to provide family support, the development of resource centres and other things. The question is, do these services that I've listed fit our analysis of what family support is going to be needed in, for example, Oxfordshire? If not, what do we have to do about it?

New Forms of Service and Provider

One of the questions raised in my mind by the research studies, and although it may seem a small thing it is important, was whether we always employ the right type of staff—not in terms of quality, but in terms of horses for courses. Some of the research, for example, showed that people attending family centres wanted befriending, relief from their children occasionally, advice, reassurance—all that sort of thing. That does not necessarily require a professionally qualified social worker. It may be a different form of animal that we need to appoint and some of the thinking nationally about family centres may be getting onto the wrong track. There is a school of thought that all family centre staff need to be social workers which, in my view, is actually dangerous. My view is that in the future there is going to be a great differentiation in what services are provided and who provides them and we must not assume that the core background to everything is social work.

Impact of Other Agencies

Another point I want to make is about the effects other agencies have on our corporate intention to try and provide family support services. If we take the community health services as an example, it is quite clear that health visiting, the availability of psychologists, different forms of therapy, specialist help for disabled children are all key parts of the provision for families in need with children in need. Part of my job as director is to try and work out how to negotiate the provision of those things. It can be incredibly difficult to get all these agencies to synchronise their activities, and it is equally frustrating when they will not do so. I am bothered about the way community health services are declining on the vine.

Then we must not forget that we are talking about implementing the Children Act just as local education authorities are implementing the educational reforms. That means, for example, local management of schools and an increase in the number of children excluded from school and what follows for childcare policy, particularly when some of those excluded are teenagers in our care in our children's homes who, if they're excluded from school, are getting into trouble. One sometimes finds an ethos of defeatism in the education authority—'Well, it's up to the schools now, we can't do anything, if we press them they'll opt out'. The different ethos between two separate departments of a council prevents policy synchronisation in respect of the under-fives or under-eights. The policies no longer necessarily stack up together. Housing is another example where social services departments may be picking up the remnants or fragments of bad housing policies.

It is sometimes assumed that the social services department equals hell and the voluntary sector equals heaven. Let nobody assume that the voluntary sector is heaven. They are as competitive as anybody else, working across each other, not synchronising with each other, not marketing their wares well. We all have to look at what the needs are, what strengths we have that we can play to, and if that means re-focussing our arrangements with each other, then we must be prepared to do it. I hope there will be an emerging knowledge about how to have service agreements and contracts with each other.

There is an issue to do with old professionalisms, new professionalisms and elitism. For example, in thinking about how different professionals do or do not work particularly well together or with non-professional colleagues, we know the stories about health colleagues or teachers or psychologists and what they all think of each other. All the little games that go on and the little elitisms that exist are really not terribly helpful to the families we are talking about. Models such as Newpin, which break down this 'professionalism' and promote a different way of working which is more oriented to users, are what we want to know more about.

Resources
My next point concerns money. Demand is exceeding supply, and there is also an effect from the problems of other agencies that I have already mentioned. The decline in Oxfordshire's community health services, particularly in the case of psychology, has led to the social services department having to employ its own psychologists. We are, it feels to me sometimes, at the end of the ripple effects of all sorts of legislation and one of the things that influences my thinking about the future is whether in fact we should be trying to create social services versions of sticking plaster to stick over other people's cracks.

In thinking about money, it may be that in the long term there could be pay-offs by developing family support, for example there may be fewer children coming into care. It may very well be that there are financial pay-offs in further home closures to pay for family support development. But, for this, one needs front end financing which goes over three or four years until one gets to the pay-off. The problem about the situation we work in is that, as a director, I do not know my budget until two months before the beginning of the financial year. One director I know had two million pounds worth of growth this year. Wonderful—but last year she had two million pounds worth of cuts. Now that is financial nonsense in terms of service planning and giving stability to an organisation.

Research into Practice
I have already said, but I want to re-emphasise, that a lot more attention needs to be given to how we convert research outputs into practice. For example, there is some excellent material in Patterns and Outcomes (DH, 1991), and also in the chapters in this book, which ought to inform our thinking about the structure of services. The trouble, to me as a layman, is the unmanageable way in which research findings are presented. I believe we need to think more carefully about how one commissions end-pieces of work to make sure that the best learning and research gets transmitted into practice very fast, in practical terms, in the form of tools that are useful. Every time, perhaps, the Department of Health commissions research in the future they ought to commission into it a requirement for an end product: the operational tools to go with the final research report. Similarly, in social services departments (and I can only speak for my world) evaluation is not part of the ethos. We go along developing new schemes, new ideas, new services, but we need also to build a systematic process of evaluation into it.

A School for Management
In this country we lack a social services management school. There is a King's Fund for the health service. Various professions have different schools. Where are the mechanisms for senior managers in social services departments to get pulled out of the humdrum day, to pick up learning, to convert it into management tools and put it back into practice? These mechanisms just do not exist, and that is important when one realises that in the last four years there has been a sixty per cent turnover of directors of social services. Lower down in our organisations there has been an equally large draining of experienced people. If one thinks of the re-organisations of social services departments over the past ten years and the experience that has gone out, it does not surprise me sometimes that we are experiencing problems at the moment.

Conclusion

To sum up the points I have made, firstly, I wonder if social services departments should be providing sticking plaster services when other agencies should be doing things better. Secondly, I stress the need for new types of worker, clearer focuses of services and a better understanding of what we are trying to achieve. Thirdly, there is the need to develop research and evaluation which feeds back into practice and management. Fourthly, we need clearer messages from partners such as voluntary agencies about what their discrete areas of specialism are and what they want to develop.

Overall, despite the problems that we always end up rehearsing, I do actually feel quite optimistic about the potential for the future, but it is going to require a lot more work and thinking, and systems that perhaps at the moment we do not have.

Reference

Department of Health (1991). *Patterns and Outcomes in Child Placement.* London: HMSO.

APPENDIX 1

Report of Seminar Workshops

TOPIC 1: In a partnership to create and maintain family support provision, what should be the particular contributions of local authority and health services and the voluntary sector, including small local groups?

Members of Group

Jan Pahl, Leader   Ruth Gardner
Peter Barclay   Tilda Goldberg
Antony Cox   Rupert Hughes
David Crook   Christine Puckering
Roy Fryer   Jane Tunstill

Summary of Discussion by Jan Pahl

This group was concerned with four main issues:

1. The service providers mentioned in the question
There was concern about the links between health and social services, and between the statutory and voluntary sector. Different organisational cultures must not be disregarded. Some local authorities are reluctant to support innovative schemes, such as Home Start; many are unwilling to give the degree of financial security which voluntary organisations require to plan ahead. On the health side, the illness-related voluntary organisations can play a valuable role, but again their funding can be neglected (some health professionals think that voluntary organisations are staffed entirely by unpaid volunteers). Health professionals, especially general practitioners and health visitors, may need training to understand the nature of family support and the various forms provision can take.

2. **Other relevant service providers**
The social security system is in many ways the bedrock of family support. Members of the group were very concerned about maintaining or increasing the levels of income support and child benefit and about restoring income support to 16-18 year olds. The group also expressed concern about the failure of the Social Fund to meet the needs of families. The education system is also a crucial source of support to families. The group deplored the fact that recent changes had created perverse incentives which make it easier for schools to exclude difficult children.

3. **The impact of the contract culture**
The demand for contracts between statutory and voluntary sectors can create difficulties; especially for small voluntary organisations, drawing up contracts can occupy disproportionate amounts of time and energy. It is important that purchasers in social services departments, and commissioners in health authorities work together; some areas, such as Tyneside and Westminster, have developed joint commissioning consortia. Joint planning and jointly held budgets can reduce the number of agencies with which a particular voluntary agency has to negotiate.

4. **The need for both diversity and co-ordination**
Diversity has to be allied with some overall sharing of information. Users should be able to move about between services and should not be tied to particular sectors by lack of information about other possibilities. The voluntary sector is particularly valuable in providing services which empower and do not stigmatise: some elected members have a very paternalistic attitude to families—one M.P. recently said to an ex-director of social services that all the children in single parent families should be taken into care. The primary health care team, and in particular the general practitioner, can play a valuable co-ordinating role. Some regional health authorities are setting out guidelines for commissioning child health services and it is important that these get through to the right services.

TOPIC 2: The Children Act requires local authorities to give due consideration to race, religion, culture and language: how should this inform the planning, delivery and evaluation of family support services?

Members of Group

Ratna Dutt, Leader
David Berridge
Jane Gibbons
Peter Maddocks
Ivan Limmer
Wendy Rose
Alvin Schorr
Ian Valender

Daphne Statham, Leader
Paul Davies
Frances Gosling
Sally Johnson
Adele Jones
Michael Leadbetter
Maggie Mills
Amanda Owen
L. F. Took
Chris Willy

Summary of Discussion by Jane Gibbons

Three principal issues concerned the groups:

1. Concepts of 'race', 'culture'

The discussions acknowledged that these concepts made many members feel uncomfortable. The concept of 'race', for example, carried an unpleasant association with the idea of placing people into categories that were based on pseudo-science and unacceptable ideology.

However, it was agreed that, in the context of the Children Act, the concept was 'shorthand' for ensuring that issues to do with significant differences, for example in language and cultural preferences that applied to anglo-saxons or celts as well as to black people, are taken account of in the delivery of services.

The concept was particularly useful in that it drew attention to racism, and the way racism affects the perception of cultural differences. i.e. 'Race', in the context of the Act, was a useful term in so far as it defined those who suffered racism.

2. Cultural issues affecting service delivery

Discussion turned to the issue of how one might ensure sensitivity to different cultural aspirations in the way services are delivered.

It was stressed that the welfare of the child is paramount under the Act. Within that perspective, cultural differences must be accepted and valued. But there may be difficulties for social services departments in taking on board perspectives of different cultural groups, especially if values surrounding family life are different. In struggling with these difficulties, it was felt that those responsible for delivering services need to be explicit about diversity and learn to understand and value it **within the framework of equal opportunities policies.**

3. Meaning of 'due consideration'

How can we operationalise 'due consideration'? i.e. What kinds of policy and practice would represent 'due consideration' to cultural differences?

The following issues were identified:

- Agencies need to start with organisational values being made explicit in a formal statement of policy. This belief statement provides a kind of benchmark, something to come back to, against which individual policies and decisions can be checked. This belief statement needs to be drawn up in consultation with minority cultural/religious groups and the effect on other agencies also needs to be considered (i.e. Will other agencies be expected to subscribe to the same belief statement?)

- Authorities have to define the target communities and what is to count as 'in need'. They need to take into account, through a formal consultation process, different perspectives of different groups in this process, as well as paying attention to structural determinants of 'need'; and then design services, preferably in an inter-agency forum which also includes strong consumer representation.

- The labour force should reflect the composition of the population, rather than aiming at an exact matching of individuals (same-race client and social worker in every case) in the delivery of services. Minority groups should be fairly represented at all levels in the organisation.

- There needs to be awareness that the provision of services can reflect the way in which problems are socially constructed (cf earlier comments on racism). e.g. Black people more likely to receive services for schizophrenia; children with mixed ethnic background over-represented in care. There is a need for ethnic monitoring to show this up.

- Rather than just retreat to segregated services, authorities need to consider how to make provision welcoming to different groups e.g. by language provision, specific issues, food, look of rooms etc. However there must be provision for special needs of cultural groups e.g. groups at risk for sickle sell anaemia need specific health education.

- There must be honesty about what the local authority can and can't/won't do. Ability to meet material needs is severely limited. 'Empowerment' may not extend very far. An example was given of a user group who took a door off its hinges because they didn't see why only staff should go through a door labelled to keep others out. The staff were not prepared to give up their power to do this.

• There needs to be training for users as well as providers of services if user participation is to become a reality.

TOPIC 3: How can service users be incorporated into the planning, management, delivery and evaluation of family support services?

Members of Groups

Bob Holman, Leader	Jabeer Butt, Leader
Erica de'Ath	Roger Bullock
Margaret Harrison	Carolyn Davies
Andrea Hickman	John Dearnley
Anne Jenkins	Joe Howsam
Simon Payne	Judith Kettle
Andrea Pound	Alastair Pettigrew
Paul Sutton	Allan Watson
June Thoburn	Angela Williams
	Teresa Smith

Summary of Discussion by Jabeer Butt

This is a summary of the above workshop held as part of the seminar on Family Support and the Children Act at the National Institute for Social Work.

The aim of the workshop was to explore this topic through an examination of the participants' understanding of what was meant by user involvement and also how user involvement could play a part in fostering what was good about existing practice in the provision of family support services and overcoming some of the problems that may exist. As the time was limited and the topic necessitates greater attention we were able only to partially explore user involvement in the planning, management, delivery and evaluation of family support services. Furthermore, with the limited attention paid to user involvement by the speakers and the varying interpretation of what was meant by user involvement throughout the day, the workshop was less structured than may have otherwise been possible.

It was clear that there was not necessarily just one interpretation of what was meant by user involvement or what it involved. Nor was it necessarily a useful thing. One participant suggested that while user involvement may be useful in certain circumstances, it was not always the case; for example there was little need for user involvement in the running of British Rail. What was more important was for British Rail to ensure that the trains run on time.

Some elements of user involvement were highlighted:

Knowing what the product was. What could be expected of it. What the outcomes should be or the standards that must be achieved.

It involved putting pressure on funding through pressure groups or key people.

It involved complaints procedure and the right to redress. One that works, but doesn't mean that they will get their revenge. User involvement was also about responsibility.

Consultation and feed-back on quality of services. There was a need to empower users and allow them to transmit their views to the service provider. The question is how to do it without being patronising?

There was some discussion as to what was good about family support services.

It was acknowledged that any approach adopted needed to build upon existing and potential strengths of family support services.

Also we must recognise that the family can be considered as a wide range of people.

There was also a question as to whether the costs of family support services meant that it was a cheaper option.

Existing good practice needed to be added to by respect for families/individual cultures and life styles.

In discussing some of the problems with family support services a number of issues were raised:

There was some debate as to what constituted a family.

Also a danger with family support services was the possibility of losing the focus on the child.

A question was also raised as to who defines what the support is? Is it the user or provider/purchaser?

In any action that was developed there was a need to carry out monitoring and evaluation from start of provision of service onwards.

There were also the issues of quality and value for money and the role of users in ensuring both.

With the development of user involvement there was the question of who owns the service.

Some concluding remarks were that:

Definitions of user involvement may vary depending on context.

Definitions should be grounded in policies/philosophies of services.

Different models of family support services may dictate different forms of user involvement.

There was a need to make the delivery of services an active process for the user.

The workshop concluded on the note that there was the possibility that better outcomes could be achieved with user involvement.

TOPIC 4: What are the two greatest obstacles preventing local authorities from extending family support provision? How might they be overcome?

Members of Group

Pauline Hardiker, Leader	David Lovell
Cathy Baines	J. K. Murdock
Stephen Barber	David Swaysland
Christopher Cloke	R. H. Sykes

Summary of Discussion by Pauline Hardiker

Initial Discussion
The group enumerated several obstacles which might influence the
nature and effectiveness of family support services: resources;
priorities; calculation of SSAs; political and community mandates;
legislation in the face of changing political priorities; the difference
between local authority and central government budgeting time
scales (former shorter); the often arbitrary and unhelpful distinctions
made between prevention and protection in child care; the
temptation to pathologise families under stress rather than
recognising the normality of difficulties in child rearing, for which
family support services are often appropriate; the difficulties in
demonstrating the effectiveness of these services, given that they are
rarely conceptualised and operationalised in helpful or realistic
ways.

Construction of Argument
The group then identified and selected from the above issues two
major obstacles for consideration.

1. Identifying and targeting family support services
Under the Act, the general preventive duty is broader than in S1 of
the C.C.A. 1980, which was negative—written in terms of keeping
children out of care rather than promoting their welfare. But the
duty is owned to a restricted group of children (i.e. 'children in
need'). One means of addressing this complex issue is for local
authorities to formulate clear policies which identify:

(a) the philosophy and value base of family support services;

(b) strategic objectives: these will identify local authority-wide
    services and those provided through the mixed economy of
    welfare in relation to the requirements of populations and early
    risk groups of children in need; then the need to target services
    in relation to children and families on the threshold of
    breakdown or 'in accommodation' or 'in care'; the aim of the
    latter service is to restore children and families to more
    universalist and community-based provisions.

(c) implementation procedures: these will provide guidelines for
    practice and policy plus monitoring devices for every level and
    type of family support services.

2. Another obstacle is the **failure to affirm and appreciate the
    nature and effectiveness of family support services** in local
    authorities, largely because levels and targets are treated in
    rather too homogeneous a way. It was suggested that data from
    'baskets of authorities' (method of the Audit Commission) might
    be produced regularly for monitoring, comparative and
    evaluation purposes. The criteria for provision outlined by the In
    Need Implementation Group in relation to the 'reasonable
    authority', the 'reasonable manager', the 'reasonable worker'
    and the 'reasonable parent' could provide a starting point. Such
    methods could highlight good policies and practices but also
    comparative shortfalls in the provision and extension of family
    support services. Stress would again be given to the importance
    of local authority-wide services, the mixed economy of welfare,
    the interprofessional and inter-agency collaboration.

Conclusions

Interventions (social work methods and packages of service etc.) will
need to be linked up much more tightly in relation to the philosophy
and strategic objectives underpinning family support for children in
need. Demonstrating effectiveness through evaluating provision in
this way is one of the best means of extending family support
services.

APPENDIX 2

Further Reading

Cox, A. D., Puckering, C., Pound, A., Mills, M. & Owen, A. L. (1990). *The Evaluation of a Home Visiting and Befriending Scheme: Newpin*. Unpublished Report to Department of Health.

Department of Health (1991). *The Children Act 1989: Guidance and Regulations. Volume 2: Family Support, Day Care and Educational Provision for Young Children*. London: HMSO.

Family Rights Group (1991). *The Children Act 1989: Working in Partnership with Families—A Training Pack*. London: HMSO.

Gardner, R. (1992). *Preventing Family Breakdown*. London: National Childrens Bureau.

Gibbons, J., Thorpe, S. & Wilkinson, P. (1990). *Family Support and Prevention: Studies in Local Areas*. London: HMSO.

Hardiker, P., Exton, K. & Barker, M. (1991). *Policies and Practice in Preventive Child Care*. Aldershot: Gower.

Holman, B. (1988). *Putting Families First: Prevention and Child Care: A Study of Prevention by Statutory and Voluntary Agencies* Basingstoke: Macmillan.

In Need Implementation Group (1991). *The Children Act and Children's Needs: Make It the Answer not the Problem*. London: National Council for Voluntary Child Care Organisations.

Packman, J. and Jordan, B. (1991). The Children Act: looking forward, looking back. *British Journal of Social Work* 21, 315-327.

Printed in the United Kingdom for HMSO
Dd.295530 C8 12/92